FOR SALE

BY OWNER

LOUIS GILMORE

REVISED AND UPDATED FOR THE 1990s

A FIRESIDE BOOK
PUBLISHED BY SIMON & SCHUSTER INC.
NEW YORK   LONDON   TORONTO   SYDNEY   TOKYO

FIRESIDE
SIMON & SCHUSTER BUILDING
ROCKEFELLER CENTER
1230 AVENUE OF THE AMERICAS
NEW YORK, NEW YORK 10020

DESIGNED BY DIANE STEVENSON, SNAP • HAUS GRAPHICS
MANUFACTURED IN THE UNITED STATES OF AMERICA

1   3   5   7   9   8   6   4   2   PBK.

LIBRARY OF CONGRESS CATALOGING IN PUBLICATION DATA

GILMORE, LOUIS
    FOR SALE BY OWNER.

    "A FIRESIDE BOOK."
    1. HOUSE SELLING, I. TITLE.
HD1379.G54   1989   333.33'8'0688   88-33459
ISBN 0-671-67939-2 PBK.

WITH THANKS
agnes, bonnie, frank, ann, sue,
joan, louis, margaret,
and tom

CONTENTS

INTRODUCTION

Every year thousands of homeowners across the country sell their homes without a real estate agent and pocket the cream of their sale—the real estate commission. These successful sellers have searched for, and found, the know-how to sell their own homes. They have challenged and overcome a complex and expensive system that forces most people to deal with a real estate agent and pay up to several thousands of dollars in commission. To most home sellers, however, the system is filled with mystery. They are compelled to conform to the system and be dependent upon it because they can't take the time to figure it out.

This book will clear up that mystery. It will show you, in a step-by-step approach, how you can sell your own home without a real estate broker. You *can* come out on top of the system and save hundreds or thousands of dollars in the process.

The entire system of home transfer in this country is one of the most costly exchange mechanisms to be found anywhere. The combination of brokerage fees and other transfer expenses take a huge toll from the seller. By far the largest and most obvious of these fees is the brokerage commission (which in some cities is now running as high as 7 percent of the selling price).

After paying a 6 or 7 percent commission, plus several hundred dollars in other transfer expenses, will the broker receive more cash from the sale than you will? Is the commission more than the buyer's downpayment? Do you have to take a loss, or price your house so high it has to move slowly? Does it represent all or almost all of the profit in your sale? Are you *losing* the downpayment on a larger home? Is it your key to a better neighborhood or a better start on retirement?

If you examine the steps in a home sale, you will find several distinct and separate parts almost all undertaken by the real estate broker.

1. Establishing the "market value" and asking price
2. Preparing advertising material
3. Advertising the house
4. Showing the house
5. Preparing a contract
6. Obtaining financing for the buyer
7. Ordering a title examination
8. Closing the transaction

Some of these services can be purchased from other professionals and the balance can be performed competently by the average home owner. The large number of homes transferred every year without a broker testifies to this fact.

Look at the possible savings for the owner who divides these services into parts, purchases some, and performs others himself.

1. A professional residential appraiser (the kind used by banks and savings and loan associations) establishes the "fair market value" of the owner's home. (Chapter 1).

2. The owner prepares his house for showing by repairing, painting, and cleaning where necessary. He enhances its condition and makes selling easier and faster. (Chapter 2).
3. The owner prepares a "listing sheet," a newspaper advertisement, and buys a "For Sale by Owner" sign. (Chapter 3).
4. The owner distributes his "listing sheet," places his newspaper advertisement, and positions his sign. (Chapter 4).
5. The owner shows his house to prospective buyers. (Chapter 5).
6. The owner, working with a bank or savings and loan officer, helps the buyer with financing. (Chapter 6).
7. A lawyer, with experience in home sales, draws up a sales contract, obtains and interprets evidence of title, and closes the transaction. (Chapter 7).

What does the home owner spend in addition to some of his own time? A written appraisal report will vary according to your location and size of your house, but should range from $150 to $200. Out-of-pocket expense for printing advertising materials and purchasing a sign should cost approximately $70.

A newspaper advertising program can cost anywhere from $200 to $1,000 depending on the extent of the program, newspaper advertising rates, and the length of time required to sell the house.

A competent lawyer will take care of many of the details involved in a home sale, be a depository of the earnest money, and explain local business practices in a home sale. This service will normally not exceed 1 percent of the sale price and usually will be around ½ of 1 percent for a $150,000 house.

Typical costs for a $150,000 suburban house that sells in a reasonable length of time are summarized as follows:

Appraiser	$175
Advertising material	$70
Newspaper campaign	$600
Lawyer's fee	$750
	$1,595

In this hypothetical situation, the owner's out-of-pocket expense for selling the house "By Owner" is $1,595. (The owner probably would have paid a legal fee even if he had sold the house through a broker. Some brokers also charge an additional expense, over the 6 percent commission rate, for advertising.) Compare this cost with a brokerage commission of 6 percent of the selling price. On the $150,000 house, the commission at 6 percent is $9,000 versus a cost of $1,595 to the owner who sells his house himself. That's a $7,405 savings that goes into the owner's pocket. Calculate the savings on your house!

What have you done to save yourself this sum? You hired an appraiser, you photographed your house, and prepared a "listing sheet" and "fact sheet" on the forms provided in the Appendix to this book. You prepared and placed newspaper ads for six to eight weeks. You showed your house. You answered the telephone and made appointments. You put on your selling hat and sold something you know better than anyone else . . . your home and your neighborhood. You worked with a bank or savings and loan officer to help the buyer with financing. You hired a competent lawyer to close your sale.

What did you save? $20,000? $17,000? $14,000? $10,000? $7,400? $5,000? or even $3,000?

Only you can decide what value your savings have. But the thousands of home owners who do it every year believe it is worth the effort. What can you do with $7,400? Buy new furniture? Savings for a college education? Hawaii? How about $3,000? How long did it take you to put away your last $3,000?

Selling your own home is not always an easy task. But look at some factors that are operating in your favor. First, you bought the home you are living in . . . you were once a buyer. You looked and shopped carefully and then made your decision to buy. You may now be looking for a replacement home. You can identify with buyers and their needs. You have a special knowledge of your neighborhood and its conveniences because you live there. You are probably an effective communicator. An enormous share of the population is involved in selling activities, if not directly in selling a product, then in selling themselves or their ideas.

You are more motivated than anyone else (even a broker) to sell *your* house. Your stakes are higher. You *can* develop the confidence that you are following the road to success in your selling effort. Many others have taken the path before you, confident that they could prepare themselves adequately for success, and many have been successful. This book and the experts you hire can make selling your own home a satisfactory and rewarding experience—and help you pocket the cream of your sale!

CHAPTER 1

FOR SALE

HOW TO SET THE RIGHT PRICE ON YOUR HOUSE

BY OWNER

Pricing your house is the first and probably the most important step you will take in selling your house. It is essential that you carefully consider the effects of either underpricing or over-pricing.

UNDERSTAND THE EFFECTS OF UNDERPRICING

Underpricing may result in a quick sale, but may also result in a substantial dollar loss to you. Simply put, if your house has a fair market value of $150,000 and you set the price at $140,000, you have "left $10,000 on the table." This can be an expensive mistake for you and a gift to the bargain hunter.

In addition to leaving money on the table, underpricing may place house buyers on guard wondering what's wrong with the "bargain house being dumped on the market."

UNDERSTAND THE EFFECTS OF OVERPRICING

The normal reaction to this fear of underpricing is to overprice. Most sellers have a tendency to be apprehensive and inflate the value of their house. They want to be certain the price is high enough to avoid the mistake of under-pricing and also high enough to leave room for negotiation. It can be just as expensive a mistake to overprice as to underprice.

If there are a number of similar houses for sale in your neighborhood, the best buy among them will usually be the first to sell. The overpriced house will probably remain on the market for a discouraging length of time. Not only will many good prospects bypass the overpriced house, but the house itself will probably gain a reputation among buyers as an "untouchable." Prospects will comment that "there must be something wrong with this house if it has been on the market for such a long period of time!" They will avoid overpriced houses because they will conclude that a sound value isn't being offered, and the path to closing your sale will be paved with much harder dealing.

Remember that the buyer's lender (almost every house is financed) is going to appraise the house. If the lender is being asked to make a fair loan and the price doesn't represent a fair market value, the loan probably won't be granted. If the buyer can't get a loan on the house he probably will be able to back out of the purchase contract. When this happens you may have wasted several weeks of your valuable time.

Your ultimate goal in setting the price on your house is to neither underprice nor overprice, but to establish a "fair market value" at which you can expect to find a qualified buyer within a reasonable period of time. A "fair market value" price tells the buyer that you are in the market to do business fairly. It is an essential part of your communications with the market and with your ultimate buyer. Your sale will be faster and smoother if your asking price is "in the ball park."

BEWARE OF YOUR SUBJECTIVITY

Several "do-it-yourself" techniques for setting a price on your house will be explained later in this chapter, but before you undertake setting the price you must understand the factors involved. The primary problem you will encounter in setting your own price is your "subjectivity."

"Subjectivity" involves your reliance on a positive or negative sentimental attachment to your property, which may result in either overpricing or underpricing. An error in either direction may cause you to suffer a financial loss.

No matter how qualified you may think you are to follow several logical steps and then arrive at what you consider to be the right price for your house, it is still *your* house. You may have lived in your house for many years and may have raised your children there. You still picture your children laughing and running through its rooms. You've spent many days painting and decorating both inside and out. You've read *Plants Are Like People* and every bush, tree, flower, and shrub has a name and a word of encouragement—what a landscaping job—and done with your own hands!

Sentimental attachments such as these make it impossible for you to be totally objective when viewing your house as a mere commodity to be bargained and sold in the competitive marketplace. It would be somewhat like asking for "objectivity" from a proud father either judging a beauty contest in which his daughter is one of the contestants, or serving as plate umpire in a Little League baseball game where his son is pitching.

This positive sentimental attachment to your house may result in substantial overpricing. Your house may remain on the market for an inordinate length of time.

The reverse may also be true. You may have had unpleasant experiences with your neighbors. One of your children may have been injured in the backyard. These or other negative events may result in a tendency to underprice your house just to be rid of it. You may have an unnecessary loss if you sell your house under these conditions.

You must also recognize your limited knowledge of market conditions. You may know the *asking prices* of houses on your block, but you may not be familiar with the *actual selling prices* of the houses *recently sold* in your neighborhood. You need access to accurate market conditions to properly price your house.

HIRE A QUALIFIED APPRAISER

Because you may have a tendency to be subjective and because you may not be familiar with existing market conditions, it is recommended that you seek the advice of a qualified real estate appraiser. His sole purpose is to give you a fair and honest opinion concerning the "fair market value" of your house. His appraisal will not be clouded by subjectivity. He will review values in terms of land prices, local building costs, existing market conditions and the special features of your house to arrive at the "fair market value." He will be trained to analyze these facts objectively and according to standard appraisal techniques.

He will be able to answer difficult questions such as: How much more should I ask because I have a swimming pool or greenhouse? Maybe nothing. Some buyers consider swimming pools a nuisance due to the required upkeep; others consider them a safety hazard, especially if there are small children in the family. How much more will I get for my house if I tear out my obsolete kitchen and install a modern one with the latest appliances and conveniences? These are difficult questions to answer unless you have specialized knowledge and experience.

There are several important factors to consider when selecting your appraiser. The man you select should not simply be an appraiser but rather an *experienced, professional, independent, residential real estate appraiser.* Each of these words preceding "appraiser" has special meaning to you.

The appraiser you select should specialize in *residential* real estate. Like many other professionals, real estate appraisers tend to specialize. Some appraisers restrict their work to appraising commercial property, such as office buildings and shopping centers. Some specialize in farm appraisals.

The appraiser you select should be *independent.* His primary business should be appraisal of residential property for a fee. His independence in your transaction should be one of your primary reasons for hiring him. Preferably he should not be associated with a real estate brokerage firm. An appraiser who is attached to a brokerage firm may find it difficult to be totally independent if he feels there is some possibility that you might be willing to list your house with his brokerage firm. You may find yourself faced with a strong sales effort to enter into a listing agreement. While the appraiser attached to a brokerage firm may be competent and knowledgeable in his field, he may also be tempted to overvalue your house to get the listing, believing that later the sales agent can get you to sell at a lower price.

The appraiser you select should be a *professional.* He should be an expert in his field who devotes full time to making formal appraisals of real estate values. He should have specialized skills, knowledge and experience. He should be a member of one or more national appraisal societies.

The largest of the national appraisal societies is the American Institute of Real Estate Appraisers (AIREA). The

AIREA has local chapters throughout the United States, conducts several schools for appraisers and sponsors lectures on various appraisal topics. The primary aim of the AIREA is to set a standard of conduct and service for its members and to publish procedures for accurate appraisal practices and principles. Once designated a full member in the AIREA, the appraiser uses the designation "M.A.I." (Member of American Institute) behind his name.

There are other national appraisal societies, such as the Society of Residential Appraisers (S.R.A.); the American Society of Appraisers (A.S.A.); and the American Society of Farm Managers and Rural Appraisers (A.R.A.). Any of the members of these organizations, as well as an appraiser who has a membership in a state appraisal society, may be qualified by education, training, and experience to appraise your house.

The appraiser you select should be *experienced*. It is preferable to hire an appraiser who has practiced for several years in your city. Many larger cities have specific areas of the city in which appraisers specialize. If you live in the southern area of your city it is advisable to find an appraiser who has appraisal experience in that specific area of the city.

Your banker or savings and loan officer will probably refer you to an appraiser if you request help. You will also find many appraisers listed in the Yellow Pages. By following the guidelines indicated above you should have no difficulty selecting a man qualified to appraise your house.

UNDERSTAND THE APPRAISER'S JOB

You are hiring the appraiser for a fixed fee to perform a specific job. He will do exactly what you request. You should be specific in your request that he provide you with a written appraisal specifying the "fair market value" of your house. Indicate that the purpose of the appraisal is to help sell your house on the open market.

Appraisers are requested to appraise property for other reasons: mortgage loans, insurance, taxes, condemnation, or inheritance. The appraiser will approach his appraisal differently depending on the purpose of the appraisal. If asked to make the appraisal for mortgage loan purposes, he will not only estimate the market value of the property but also rate the property risks involved in making the loan. If asked to value the property for fire insurance he will be trying to protect the insured in the event of total loss.

His specific purpose in appraising your house must be to establish a "fair market value." The American Institute of Real Estate Appraisers defines market value as "the price expectable if a reasonable time is allowed to find a purchaser and if both seller and prospective buyer are fully informed." Another definition by the Institute is "the price at which a willing seller would sell and a willing buyer would buy, neither being under abnormal pressure." The fundamental principles in these definitions are (1) the transaction must be voluntary, (2) the parties involved in the transaction must be normal users who are well-informed, (3) adequate time has passed to allow for proper testing of your house in a competitive marketplace, and (4) there are purchasers in the market who have the financial ability to purchase the property on the basis of financing currently available.

At this point it is important that you realize the difference between "market price" and "market value." "Market price" is defined as the dollar amount that is paid in a transaction for a specific property. "Market value" refers to the prices that buyers are currently paying in your market. Value may be higher or lower than price. Your house may have a specific market value set by the appraiser under the definition of market value, but this does not mean that it will sell at that exact level. You may raise your price well above the appraiser's market value and find a purchaser who is ignorant of market conditions, or under undue stress, and who will purchase your house at a price over the market value.

The appraiser cannot predict with absolute accuracy the "price" of your house. He can only give his best professional opinion of the "value" of the house. Only by placing your house on the market and receiving one or more offers will you actually determine what is described rather academically as "value." Only when you close the sale will you have determined the "price."

In preparing his appraisal report the appraiser will determine the type of area in which you live: subdivision, rural, or urban. He will gather an overall impression of whether the market considers your area of the city good, average, fair, or poor. He will note the neighborhood trend, whether it is appreciating, stable, or declining. He will record the average age of the houses in your area and the general type of construction in the neighborhood. He will analyze some of the so-called "intangible qualities" that may interest a potential buyer (proximity of public transportation, reputation of local schools, cultural activities, the location of parks and shopping centers, and other factors that would tend to increase or decrease the value of your house).

The appraiser will gather site data relating to your landscaping, driveway, type of lot and roof, exterior walls, porch, breezeways, guttering, and other features. In each case he will indicate both the good and bad characteristics.

He will concentrate on construction details and note any obvious problems related to the foundation, basement, electricity, air conditioning, plumbing, heating, chimney, or roof. Some of these items are important features that may be in demand in specific areas of the country, for example, central air conditioning, extra quality insulation, or a certain type of heating.

He will then study the interior of each room, concentrating on the overall quality and condition of the walls, floors, and woodwork. He will note requirements for repairs and remodeling and look for the existence of termites or dry rot. He will pay specific attention to the kitchen to determine whether it is obsolete, semimodern, or modern, and note the type of appliances and built-ins. He will note the condition of the tiling and plumbing fixtures since the condition of bathrooms will be of particular interest to buyers.

The appraiser's considerations are elaborated above to give you some understanding of the detailed factors that he will take into account in making his appraisal. For your appraisal to be as accurate as possible, the appraiser must view your house in the same condition as it will be viewed by prospective buyers. Chapter 2 discusses the preparations for showing your house. It is important that all repairs and maintenance be made prior to the appraiser's inspection so that he may take them into account in formulating his opinion of value. The appraiser must view the house as if he were a potential purchaser.

Inform the appraiser of all features of your house including financing. If you have a low-interest rate, long-term loan, which the buyer can assume, advise the appraiser. The discounted value of low-interest rate, long-term financing may be capitalized into savings for the buyer, and may enhance the value of your house (Chapter 6).

You should have a basic understanding of how an appraiser reaches his conclusions regarding the market value of a house. There are three approaches that appraisers generally use to appraise real estate: *income approach, cost approach,* and *market approach.*

The *income approach* is rarely used in residential appraisals since the calculation involves determining the value of the property based on the income that can be derived from ownership. Unless many of the houses in your neighborhood are frequently rented, this approach will probably not be used by your appraiser.

In the *cost approach,* the appraiser calculates the replacement cost of your house on a square-foot basis, and then deducts an amount for depreciation based on the physical and functional characteristics of your house. He adds value for other conditions such as a garage, attached buildings, or lot improvements. He then adds a value for the land. Appraisal by the cost approach can often be very precise where the houses are in a subdivision that is relatively new. For older homes, however, depreciation is sometimes difficult to measure and the subjectivity of the measurement becomes the primary weakness of this approach.

The *market approach* is frequently the most accurate appraisal method for residential property. It gives an indication of current price trends and takes into account the important influence the "market" has on the value of your house.

Many major metropolitan areas have a service that assists appraisers using the market approach. Chicago, for example, has a service that provides the appraiser with current data on house sales made throughout Chicago and its suburbs. The service indicates the address, date of sale, selling price, amount of the mortgage, and the type of financing used in purchase. A code indicates the type of house such as bungalow, Cape Cod, split-level, duplex, Georgian, French Norman, English, half-timber, contemporary, or ranch. Data is provided on age, number of square feet, type of heating, and central air conditioning. The general overall condition of the house is rated as either excellent, good, average, or fair. Kitchen details are provided for built-in oven, range, and dishwasher. The reporting service is complete, up-to-date, and a valuable asset to qualified appraisers.

The appraiser will have a good reading of asking prices by analyzing broker listings and newspaper advertisements for other houses that are currently for sale in your area. The appraiser will try to compare your house to similar houses that have recently sold. He will analyze similarity in location, lot and building size, condition and contents. He will then make adjustments for factors that differ, such as number of baths, number of bedrooms, preferential locations, and the general overall condition of your house versus comparable houses that were sold. He will also take into account changes in the housing market since the comparable houses that were sold.

If you have selected an *experienced, professional, independent, residential real estate appraiser* who properly applies the tools of his trade, his detailed written appraisal will be a valuable asset in arriving at the ''fair market value'' of your house.

APPRAISE THE HOUSE YOURSELF

Many ''By Owner'' sellers will wonder whether or not they can save the appraisal fee and appraise the house themselves. Although having an appraiser is generally recommended, it is possible for a seller to follow certain procedures and appraise his own house with a fair degree of accuracy. The accuracy depends heavily on the amount of effort put forth by the owner, his analytical ability, and the house itself.

Certain houses are easier to appraise than others. If the house is located in a newly developed subdivision where all the houses have approximately the same acreage and were built by the same builder, the appraisal task is much easier. If the houses are older and each house in the neighborhood has its own individual character, the task is much more difficult.

Certain techniques that are available to the seller appraising his own house are discussed below. While these techniques will be helpful if properly applied, the seller must also be aware of certain pitfalls.

Often the do-it-yourself oriented person has a tendency to judge the market value of his house by relying on the uneducated and uninformed opinions of friends and neighbors. Your neighbor may be happy to help you set a value on your house but, like you, he has some of the built-in subjectivity problems that were discussed earlier. He may be sentimentally attached to the oak trees lining your street or the quality of the neighborhood school where his children were educated.

Your neighbor may also tell you that the house down the street recently sold for $150,000. Since your well-informed neighbor told you that it has sold for $150,000 it would be simple enough to rely on this information and relate your price to this price. But before taking this approach, ask yourself if your neighbor is certain of the selling price. Very often what people think a house sold for and the actual closing price are somewhat different. The buyer might indicate a price less than he really paid for the house to enhance his image as an astute judge of value or a good negotiator. The departing seller, on the other hand, might indicate that he got a terrific price for this house and may puff the value. Be careful if you try to rely on "your neighbor the expert."

DEVELOP YOUR OWN MARKET DATA

One of the tools a professional appraiser has at his fingertips is current community data which gives some indication of the supply and demand factors operating in the marketplace. The fair market value for your house fluctuates over time and is responsive to changing conditions. Check with your chamber of commerce or local bank to get an indication of the typical factors that will help you judge the strength of the home market in which you must sell your house.

Increasing or decreasing activity in several areas of business may be of help: the level of retail sales, the change in savings deposits, the subdivision construction activity, the numbers of mortgage recordings, and movement of major employers in or out of the area.

Watch the activity in the housing market through the local paper, including the building of new homes in your price range. Make Sunday afternoon trips through your community and observe the number of houses for sale and the frequency of turnover. The status of a local market is difficult to judge, so be aware of your own shortcomings in making this judgment.

After determining, as best you can, whether or not you are operating in a buyer's or seller's market, check your neighborhood, or comparable neighborhoods, for houses currently listed for sale. Most of these houses will be open for inspection on Sunday afternoon or you can contact the real estate broker listing the house and make an appointment. By listing the selling price of four or five comparable houses, you will have some idea of current trends. Make certain to adjust the asking prices based on comparables such as the number of baths, number of bedrooms, lot size, location, and condition. Remember to be objective and discard subjectivity when studying these comparables.

During your market survey you may find houses comparable to yours that have recently sold. The brokerage firm that sold the houses may tell you the latest asking price but will probably not divulge the final sale price. Some states will have tax stamps recorded on the deed that will enable you to determine the sales price. Call your county courthouse to see if this can assist you. (The requirement for federal stamps has been eliminated and not all states have adopted state tax stamps.)

TALK TO THE BROKERS

Another method that may prove helpful in setting your own price is contacting four or five reputable real estate brokers operating in your local area. Request that they visit your house and provide you with a suggested asking price and selling price. Inform the brokers that you are going to attempt to sell your house yourself but will call them later if you change your mind. They may be receptive to the idea and give you their opinion of the value of your house. Record the asking price recommended by each of the brokers and take an average to arrive at an asking price.

Be prepared for the broker to try to sell you on listing your house with his firm. This is only natural since selling houses is his business. You can be certain that the broker will tell you to list with him because: "It's a nuisance to have all those people stomping through your house . . . your telephone will ring all the time and drive you crazy . . . you won't be able to find a qualified buyer yourself . . . it will take you forever to sell it yourself . . ."

Surveying the brokers often can be a reasonable approach to arriving at a market value, but this has some built-in disadvantages. Some brokers may have a tendency to inflate the value of your house in order to obtain a listing contract. They reason that since you are interested in selling your house at the highest possible price, you will select the broker that "promises" that he can *get* the highest price. Once he has obtained your written listing contract, however, and the house has been on the market for a period of time, he will then be in a position to suggest that you lower the price. As long as you realize the pitfalls, it may be helpful to contact three or four brokers and average their estimates. This method can help protect you against too high an estimate of fair market value.

You can learn from the brokers that visit your house. Ask them how they arrived at their market price and what advantages and disadvantages they see to selling your house. Don't forget, however, that in order to sell your house they must first obtain a listing contract. This requires them to sell you first on the fact that they, as brokers, can sell your house. Diplomacy dictates that they restrain from pointing to deficiencies in your handiwork around the house, at least until the listing agreement is signed. This flattery could be costly. A realistic appraisal of the situation is what you really desire.

TRY THE COMBINATION PUNCH

Although it is generally recommended that you use a professional appraiser to give you the most accurate opinion of the fair market value of your house, several other approaches have been mentioned also that will help you appraise the house yourself.

One final thought on the matter of arriving at a fair market value for your house. Why not test as many approaches as your time permits and weigh the results? You can rely most heavily on the value attributed to your house by the appraiser, but can modify this by comments of brokers or other information you may have obtained.

All of these various factors should tend to cluster around a common market value. This combination process will not have

created more difficulty for you, but instead, each approach will
tend to support the other and you will have more confidence in
your final determination of the market value.

SET YOUR FAIR MARKET VALUE

You cannot set a market "price" on your house because
the "price" can be finally determined only when your house is
sold. You must now, however, arrive at your "fair market
value" through one of the approaches discussed above. This
"value" will be the focal point around which you establish
your minimum price and your asking price. It is the market
"value" that you ultimately hope to reach by negotiation.
Then close the sale and turn your market "value" into a
market "price."

SET YOUR MINIMUM PRICE

If you made the decision to sell your present house in order
to purchase or build a new house, you have, no doubt,
investigated the cash required to purchase your new house.
Although a portion of your cash requirements may come from
your savings, the sale of your present house will probably be
contributing a major portion of the cash.

If you have an $80,000 mortgage on your present house
and require $20,000 cash from the sale to purchase your new
house, remember to consider the additional expenses of selling
your house to calculate your minimum selling price. Add the
following expenses to your minimum cash needs and you can
then set your minimum price:

Appraiser	$____
Advertising material	$____
Newspaper campaign	$____
Lawyer's fee	$____
Repairs	$____
Seller's closing costs	$____

If the above expenses add up to $5,000 you will need a minimum selling price of $135,000 to receive the $50,000 net cash you require ($80,000 mortgage plus $5,000 selling expenses plus $50,000 cash requirement equals $135,000 minimum selling price). If you had not considered these additional selling expenses you might have set your minimum selling price at $130,000 and your net cash received (if you sold at your $130,000 minimum) would have been only $45,000, or $5,000 short of your cash requirements.

You will soon enter the stage of negotiation. When a potential purchaser makes an offer, you must do one of three things: (1) accept the offer, (2) counter with a higher price, or (3) reject the offer. To make this decision an informed one, you must establish your minimum price.

The determination of this minimum selling price is not simply a mental exercise but an important part of the negotiations into which you will enter finally in determining what you will accept for your house. To be effective in any negotiation you must know your bottom limit. Remember that this minimum price is not what you think the house is worth, but rather a determination of your bottom price, below which you are not willing to negotiate.

SET YOUR ASKING PRICE

You have now established a fair market value and a minimum price. The final price which you must establish is your asking price.

Different markets have different characteristics. When you approach the counter at the supermarket to buy a can of coffee you expect to pay the price as marked on the item. When you purchase a used car you expect to negotiate with the salesman. The market for houses in this country has traditionally been a negotiating or bargaining market. Seldom does a prospective buyer expect to pay the first price that has been quoted on a house. Recognizing the fact, you must add a "negotiating amount" to your fair market value to arrive at your asking price.

The customary spread between the asking price and the ultimate sale price varies from city to city. Ask your appraiser what is "normal" in your city. Generally, adding 5 to 10 percent to the appraised market value will give you sufficient room for negotiating and will bring you somewhere close to the price that you hope to receive for your house. Remember that this is only a rule of thumb. Your goal in setting the asking price is to leave negotiating room and still stay within the market for comparable houses. Don't overdo it and end up overpricing your house.

Recall what was mentioned earlier about overpricing your house. "Time is money," especially if you have signed a contract to purchase another house or have started construction on a new house. Overinflating the asking price may scare off several prospective buyers. They anticipate a certain amount of puffery in your asking price, but if you've added 25 percent, prospective buyers may not consider viewing your house since you have priced it out of their range.

You have now established your asking price and you are ready to go to market. Don't ever talk about "asking" price anymore, it is your price—don't use "asking" in your ads. If you do, it will just emphasize to the buyer that he must negotiate. Take the stand that it is your price and try to get it. Indicate it is "firm."

Asking Price $____

Market value $____

Minimum Price $____

CHECK LIST
HOW TO SET THE RIGHT PRICE ON YOUR HOUSE

☐ UNDERSTAND THE EFFECTS OF UNDERPRICING

☐ UNDERSTAND THE EFFECTS OF OVERPRICING

☐ BEWARE OF YOUR SUBJECTIVITY

☐ HIRE A QUALIFIED APPRAISER

☐ UNDERSTAND THE APPRAISER'S JOB

☐ APPRAISE THE HOUSE YOURSELF

☐ DEVELOP YOUR OWN MARKET DATA

☐ TALK TO THE BROKERS

☐ TRY THE COMBINATION PUNCH

☐ SET YOUR FAIR MARKET VALUE

☐ SET YOUR MINIMUM PRICE

☐ SET YOUR ASKING PRICE

CHAPTER 2

FOR SALE

HOW TO PREPARE YOUR HOUSE

BY OWNER

Selling a house is a step-by-step process, whereby your own confidence in the value of your house should transmit itself to the prospective buyer. When a prospect inspects your house he should be positive that you are offering him a true value.

There are many ways that you, as the seller, can prepare your house in order to gain this confidence. Signs of care in the maintenance of your house are definite indications of pride of ownership. Fresh paint; bright, sparkling windows; crisp, clean curtains; spacious, orderly closets; and a well-manicured lawn, can all add up to a good first impression. Attention to these details and many other seemingly small details will indicate the amount of care you have invested in your house, and may give your house the competitive edge over others the prospect might have considered.

The condition of a house and its grounds can also affect the ease and speed of your selling effort. Prospects shop, investigate, and weigh value. One of the key factors they consider is condition.

MAKE A GOOD FIRST IMPRESSION

Imagine for a moment that you are the one who is house-hunting and you find your own house listed for sale.

You drive past and find it attractive. You arrange with the owner to inspect the house and find yourself driving up for your appointment. You notice the lawn has a few brown patches and requires trimming, but then "there's no such thing as a perfect house" and from the street the house is attractive.

As you walk up to the front door you examine the foundation plantings. They are a little overgrown and uncultivated, but if this were a new house it would take several hundred dollars to duplicate them.

You push the bell and nothing happens. It doesn't work. As you stand there waiting you notice the door. The paint is beginning to chip and crack. You knock and begin to look around with a more critical eye. You notice the gutters and downspouts and focus on a few rust spots seeping through the paint. You wonder how much life is left in the gutters. Looking up you spot a loose shingle and remind yourself to inspect the interior ceilings and walls for signs of water leakage. Your mood has changed from "definitely interested" to "wary and critical."

Now let's replay the scene. The seller has made a detailed inspection of his house and grounds before showing it. He has spent $15 on a bag of fertilizer and worked on the lawn for three or four weeks before offering the house. He pruned the shrubs and hired two neighborhood high school students to weed and cultivate them and trim along the walks.

The students sanded the gutters and the front door in preparation for a fresh coat of paint. The seller installed a new doorbell so that he could welcome prospects into a house that was not in need of even minor repairs. This seller's conditioning program ensures that more of the first impressions will be "definitely interested" ones, and that more buyers will want to start serious house-hunting here.

SPEND YOUR REMODELING MONEY WISELY

Most home owners believe that home remodeling is an investment. They feel they can recover in their selling price the cost of all improvements. They think *value* always equals *cost*. The plain fact is, however, that money spent on some improvements may not even return fifty cents on the dollar.

You must be aware of the *value* of various expenditures as they relate to *cost*. Spend your remodeling money wisely. Don't overvalue your remodeling costs.

Assume that you bought your house six months ago for $150,000 and installed a new furnace for $4,000. Your total cost is now $154,000. If there has been no change in the market price, can you add $4,000 to $150,000 and sell your house for $154,000? The answer is probably "no." Most people expect a furnace to be in good working order when they buy a house. They won't pay extra for what is expected.

If your kitchen is obsolete, you can spend up to about 10 percent of the value of your house for remodeling and building appliances. Within this range you may be able to recover all of your cost. If you spend more than 10 percent you risk not being able to recover your cost.

There are two ways to add a bedroom. You can convert an unfinished second floor into a bedroom at a cost of $5,000 to $7,000, or you can add a new room to the house at a cost of 25 to 30 percent more. Watch the prices of nearby new houses. Compare your expected selling price, after you add the bedroom, to the price of a new house with the same number of bedrooms. If the builders are getting less than you need in order to recover your cost, you probably shouldn't add the bedroom.

Depending on where you live, adding a full bath can cost $3,500 or more. If you now have only one bath, you may be able to recover the full cost of adding a second bath. If you now have two baths, you will be lucky to get 80 percent of your cost back if you add a third bath.

Basement recreation rooms aren't as popular as they have been in the past and they are usually very expensive to build. If your basement is completely below grade don't expect to get 100 percent of your cost back. However, if your basement opens to an outside patio or if you are improving a split-level house, you may come close to getting your money back (if you don't spend more than 5 percent to 7 percent of the value of your house).

In locations where air conditioning is a necessity, you may be able to recover up to 100 percent of your cost if you install a central air-conditioning system. In cooler climates this may not be true. You may be lucky to recover 75 percent of your cost. Window or through-the-wall air-conditioning units are cheaper, but you'll never get 100 percent of your cost back. You'll be lucky to get 50 percent.

If you live in a cool climate and you add a garage, you may get all of your money back. In warmer climates a garage may not add much value to your house.

Repainting a frame house can run $3,000 to $7,000, depending on the size of the house and the condition of the present paint. Buyers expect the paint to be in reasonably good condition. If the present condition of your paint is still reasonably good you may only recover 25 percent of what you spend for a new paint job. However, if the present condition of your paint is very poor you may recover as much as 80 percent by repainting, and you'll sell your house faster.

Remember to spend your remodeling money wisely. If you have made improvements don't overvalue them. You may not always be able to recover your full cost. Overvaluing may cause overpricing and, as a result, your house may take longer to sell.

SELL YOUR SPACE

If you are selling an older house, one of the competitive advantages that you may have over sellers of new homes is the additional space you offer for the dollar. Your prospect *must* be made aware of the space you are offering, or your house may not get a fair shake when he compares it with other houses.

Too much furniture can make a room look small. If you have a lot of furniture, or massive pieces that are out of proportion with the room, consider moving some of the furniture into storage. Rearrange your furniture to show the room sizes to their fullest advantage.

Now is the time to have your garage sale. Don't wait until your house is on the market, or until it is sold. Cleaning around items you intend to sell just makes your work that much harder. Out-of-season clothing hung in closets should be boxed and stored elsewhere. Basements and attics should be thoroughly cleaned. Seldom used items should be stored, sold, or junked. Call the Salvation Army or Goodwill Industries to pick up any items you no longer need.

Kitchen cabinets and counter tops can be a source of clutter. Remove some of your least used items from these areas and store them so you can show your space to its fullest.

PLAN YOUR RECONDITIONING EARLY

If your house is in sound structural condition and well maintained, most of your preparation work will be cosmetic. It will require no more effort than spring cleaning with an extra dose of paint and elbow grease to touch up some neglected details.

If there are repairs that you cannot undertake because of the season (roof repairs or lawn sodding) tell the prospect that you will have them done to his satisfaction between the time the contract is signed and the sale is closed.

There are certain maintenance items which have a long lead-time. Pruning may take six months to a year to show its full effect. Lawn fertilizing may take two or three weeks. A complete paint job may take three or four weeks. Timing is an important element of your planning. Start well in advance of the time you put your house on the market. Sort out those things that must be done early and then get to work!

REPAIR MAJOR ITEMS

Prospects want to be certain that the major structural and mechanical components of the house are in good working order. Certain defects will have to be repaired or you may have to sell for a lot less than your target price. These include:

1. *Termite infestation and rotten wood.* If there is any sign of termite damage have it corrected. Have a reputable termite service inspect your house and give you a clean bill of health. The report should be available to show to prospects.
2. *Cracked structure.* If any ceilings or walls have major cracks, prospects will suspect that serious structural repairs are needed. They will probably have an engineer inspect your house. Plaster and paint before your house goes on the market.
3. *Inadequate electrical wiring.* Your wiring is probably adequate if you have modern appliances such as a washer, dryer, electric stove, dishwasher, or central air conditioning. If your house isn't wired for modern

appliances, you should expect most prospects to deduct the expense of installing new electrical service from your asking price. FHA inspectors will require your wiring to conform to the building code for your city.

4. *Heating system malfunctions.* If your heating system is old, if it thumps, clanks, or bangs, have it inspected and cleaned by a heating contractor. The charge will be nominal and he will advise you of any major problems that can be anticipated. This information will be helpful in dealing with a buyer who is concerned about the condition of your heating plant.

5. *Leaky or defective plumbing.* If your pipes are old and corroded you can expect your prospects to be cautious. If you recently had a pipe blowout, the inserted new section of pipe may alert your prospect to the possibility of future plumbing failures. Have a plumbing contractor inspect your house so you will have the facts to counter your prospect's objections.

6. *Wet basement or signs of water penetration.* Basement moisture can be a perplexing problem. The presence of water in a basement does not necessarily mean the foundation walls are not tight and dry. Water occurs in basements not only from water penetration but from condensation. Make certain you correct this situation. This will be discussed in more depth later in this chapter.

INSPECT THE EXTERIOR

Begin your inspection with the exterior of your house. View your house from the street. Judge the overall condition of the front of your house including the lawn, foundation plantings, trees, fences, sidewalk, and driveway. Examine each of these features closely to determine if you need to take any action. Can the lawn be greened up with an application of fertilizer? Can it be improved by an application of weed killer? Can the condition of the foundation plantings and beds be improved by mulch? The appearance of the house will be improved if dead plants are replaced.

Examine the walk and driveway. Should the driveway be sealed? Are there any cracks or holes that could be a safety hazard to guests or prospects? Is the lawn trimmed neatly around the walks and driveways? Do shade and ornamental trees have any large dead limbs that should be removed? Are there any dead trees that should be removed?

Approach the house as if you were the prospective buyer. Check each item of maintenance immediately as it strikes your eye. Look for peeling or blistering paint, a crooked shutter, rusting gutter or downspout, cracked windowpanes, turned-up shingles, debris lodged in the gutters, winter ice overhanging the gutters, loose mortar, or a window sash in need of paint. Note each of these defects so you can return to them and make the necessary repairs.

Make a careful examination of the exterior of the house from the ground to the top of the first-floor windows. As you walk around the house, examine the foundation walls carefully to make certain there are no termite tubes running from the ground up to or along the siding. Termite tubes are the color of dried mud and will be about the thickness of your finger. If you spot any of these tubes call an exterminator at once and have your house surveyed for any possible structural damage.

Check to see if the basement window airways are cleaned and if the covers are in place and painted. Take a close look at the foundation plantings to see if they need to be fertilized or replaced. Inspect all exterior windows and doors and check the condition of the paint. Check all exterior lights to be certain they are operative.

Exterior brass work around mailboxes, doors, and lamps is an important feature of your house. Be certain these are shown to their best advantage. A couple of hours with brass polish and spray lacquer can dress them up. Examine the hardware on all exterior doors to make certain it is tight and in good working order.

Examine your garage, carport, or exterior storage area. Remember you are selling *space*. Display your storage space as attractively as possible. Signs of clutter in your garage or outside storage areas will not let a prospect judge the actual amount of space available.

Tools should be hung in a neat and orderly fashion. Be certain the garage is swept and that all hardware is tight and in working order. Check to see that light fixtures are operative. If you have an electric garage door-opener, make certain that it is in working order. If not, be sure the spring on your garage door is balanced so that the door is not difficult to open. A drop of oil on the hinges will keep them quiet.

INSPECT THE BASEMENT

The next stop on your inspection tour should be the basement. As mentioned earlier, your basement should be dry. A damp or wet basement tells the prospect a lot about what he is going to get for his money . . . extra space for extra headaches. Any prospect will know that a wet basement can mean serious foundation or drainage problems.

If your basement is damp start by trying to dry it up. Many damp basements can be dried out by wrapping the cold water pipes to eliminate condensation of moisture. Feel the pipes and examine the floor under them. If the pipes are wet, airborne water has condensed on them (like an iced drink in the summer). Wrap the pipes with a commercial wrapping that you can buy at the hardware store and you may have gone a long way toward curing the problem.

Another contributing factor to basement dampness may be an improperly vented laundry dryer. All the moisture has to go somewhere.

Condensation on walls can be part of the dampness problem. The simplest and fastest cure is to buy a dehumidifier and install it in the basement. Run it until the basement dries. This should take away any dampness or musty odors. It will not, however, remove sewer gas odors, which are a symptom of serious plumbing disorders. If you have this problem, have it professionally repaired.

More serious problems of basement dampness are poor drainage around the foundation, cracks in the floor and basement walls, leaks around pipes going through basement walls, leaks around basement windows, and plugged drains. These conditions may be symptoms of serious problems. If your house has them, you should consider consulting a waterproofing contractor to estimate the cost of repairs.

If your basement is dry, you will have a definite marketing advantage. You can point to a recreation room or storage area as evidence of confidence in your dry basement.

The basement should be broom clean and the stairway free of clutter. The stair railing leading to the basement should be tightened and strong enough to support weight. If you use your basement as a major storage area consider renting a garage to store these items until your sale is completed. It is difficult for prospects to inspect around these objects and hard to clean when it is overfilled. It is better to show a nearly empty basement than a cluttered one.

If your basement has an odor which a prospect might find

objectionable, invest ninety-nine cents in a room deodorizer. Place it in an inconspicuous place to freshen up the air.

Basement drains should be operative. Basement windows and air wells should be cleaned.

You may have to demonstrate your furnace before a prospect will sign a contract. With this in mind, have the operating instructions handy and in an envelope near the controls so the prospect can conveniently review them.

INSPECT THE INTERIOR

After you have inspected the exterior and basement, continue on your tour by inspecting each room. Look for spotted or water-stained walls, worn woodwork, scuffed floors, loose hardware, sticking windows or drawers, leaky plumbing, dripping faucets, and dim lighting.

Your inspection tour is an essential part of preparing your house for selling. To assist you in your inspection a detailed check list is provided at the end of this chapter.

Tour your house room by room and determine what should be done, depending upon the amount of time and money you want to invest in the project. Spend your time and money on those projects that will produce the most return for your efforts. This check list should only be considered as a guide. If you see other things that require repair or reconditioning, take care of them.

The check list should be used as a planning tool for reconditioning your house as well as the place to record an item of repair as the work is performed. It covers the entrances, family room, living room, dining room, kitchen, bathrooms and bedrooms. In addition check lists are provided for the areas discussed earlier: landscaping and grounds, patios and terraces, house exterior, garage, and basement.

HIRE HELP TO GET THE JOB DONE

A moderately strenuous program of house conditioning has been recommended. If you don't have the time to do all of it yourself, consider hiring someone to do the time-consuming jobs such as wall and window washing, woodwork sanding, paint scraping, waxing, polishing, sweeping, and hauling. You might be able to hire a professional cleaning service to do one or two rooms, or a professional yard maintenance company to upgrade your lawn and plantings. You will have to balance the cost of the professional services against the speed with which they work and the thoroughness of the job.

Enterprising students can often show up with a whole team and, in one afternoon, do things that would take you four weekends. Moonlighting carpenters, plumbers, and painters often are available at a reduced cost.

Get the job done! Don't underestimate the role of preparation in selling your house.

LANDSCAPING & GROUNDS

	Item to Be Done	Supplies & Equipment Needed	Cost	To Be Done By	Date

LAWN

☐ lawn condition good
☐ grass mowed
☐ edges trimmed around:
   ☐ house
   ☐ fences
   ☐ trees
   ☐ walks
   ☐ driveway
   ☐ planting beds

TREES

☐ dead limbs removed
☐ dead trees removed

FOUNDATION & PLANTINGS

☐ shrubs trimmed
☐ dead shrubs removed
☐ dead shrubs replaced
☐ overgrown shrubs trimmed

PATIOS & TERRACES

- [ ] surface smooth and clean
- [ ] no standing water
- [ ] free of storage

If porch or terrace is wood, it should be recently:

- [ ] stained or painted
- [ ] free of termites
- [ ] free of dry rot
- [ ] railings sound and secure

Item to Be Done	Supplies & Equipment Needed	Cost	To Be Done By	Date

Item to Be Done	Supplies & Equipment Needed	Cost	To Be Done By	Date

DRIVEWAY

- ☐ surface smooth
- ☐ holes patched
- ☐ asphalt recently sealed
- ☐ gravel smoothed and weeded

DECORATING FLOWERS

- ☐ interior potted flowers, bulbs, plants ready for use in:
  - ☐ entry hall
  - ☐ living room
  - ☐ kitchen
  - ☐ patio
  - ☐ other

HOUSE EXTERIOR

- [ ] recently painted
- [ ] free of blistering or peeling paint
- [ ] shutters straight
- [ ] gutters, downspouts sound, free of rust
- [ ] recently painted
- [ ] exterior lights operating
- [ ] turned-up shingles renailed
- [ ] loose mortar pointed
- [ ] exterior fixtures painted
- [ ] chimney mortar tight
- [ ] flashing secure, leak free

WINDOWS

- [ ] no cracked panes
- [ ] sashes recently painted
- [ ] work freely

AIRWAYS

- [ ] clean
- [ ] covers painted, in place

Item to Be Done	Supplies & Equipment Needed	Cost	To Be Done By	Date

BASEMENT

- ☐ structural elements sound
- ☐ no cracked wall, sagging beams
- ☐ no dry rot
- ☐ no termite infestation
- ☐ no water penetration
- ☐ no dampness
- ☐ no musty or sewer-gas odor
- ☐ no stopped-up drains
- ☐ excess storage removed
- ☐ remaining storage neat
- ☐ broom clean condition
- ☐ all lights operating

Stairway:

- ☐ free of storage
- ☐ handrail secure
- ☐ lights bright and operating
- ☐ treads tight and covering secure

Furnace:

- ☐ inspected and cleaned

Item to Be Done	Supplies & Equipment Needed	Cost	To Be Done	
			By	Date

GARAGE

- ☐ free of accumulated storage
- ☐ recently swept and orderly
- ☐ tools and equipment neatly stored
- ☐ light fixtures operating
- ☐ door opens easily and quietly
- ☐ electric door-opener works

Item to Be Done	Supplies & Equipment Needed	Cost	To Be Done By	Date

ENTRANCES

- [ ] hall light operating
- [ ] light fixture clean
- [ ] switchplate clean
- [ ] closet hardware operating
- [ ] closet light operating
- [ ] closet not overcrowded
- [ ] rugs and carpets clean, and secure against slippage
- [ ] floors waxed
- [ ] windows washed and work freely
- [ ] curtains fresh and crisp
- [ ] entry lights operating
- [ ] entry light fixtures cleaned
- [ ] mailbox recently polished
- [ ] door brass recently polished
- [ ] doorbell operating
- [ ] steps structurally sound
- [ ] if wood, free of rot
- [ ] door recently painted
- [ ] woodwork recently painted
- [ ] door hardware operating
- [ ] hinges free of squeaks

Item to Be Done	Supplies & Equipment Needed	Cost	To Be Done By	Date

FAMILY ROOM

Item to Be Done	Supplies & Equipment Needed	Cost	To Be Done By	Date
□ walls free of water stain □ wallpaper tight to walls □ walls clean □ windows freshly washed □ cracked or broken panes replaced □ curtains and drapes clean □ window sashes operate freely □ window sills clean □ woodwork recently painted, not soiled, scuffed, or marred				
□ floor recently waxed □ carpets clean, tacked down □ doors and frames clean □ recently painted □ door hardware operates free of squeaks □ furniture arranged to best show room size				

LIVING ROOM

- ☐ walls free of water stain
- ☐ wallpaper tight to walls
- ☐ walls clean
- ☐ windows freshly washed
- ☐ cracked or broken panes replaced
- ☐ curtains and drapes clean
- ☐ window sashes operate freely
- ☐ window sills clean
- ☐ woodwork recently painted, not soiled, scuffed, or marred
- ☐ floor recently waxed
- ☐ carpets clean, tacked down
- ☐ doors and frames clean
- ☐ recently painted
- ☐ door hardware operates free of squeaks
- ☐ furniture arranged to best show room size

Item to Be Done	Supplies & Equipment Needed	Cost	To Be Done By	Date

DINING ROOM

- ☐ walls free of water stain
- ☐ wallpaper tight to walls
- ☐ walls clean
- ☐ windows freshly washed
- ☐ cracked or broken panes replaced
- ☐ curtains and drapes clean
- ☐ window sashes operate freely
- ☐ window sills clean
- ☐ woodwork recently painted, not soiled, scuffed, or marred
- ☐ floor recently waxed
- ☐ carpets clean, tacked down
- ☐ doors and frames clean
- ☐ recently painted
- ☐ door hardware operates free of squeaks
- ☐ furniture arranged to best show room size

Item to Be Done	Supplies & Equipment Needed	Cost	To Be Done By	Date

KITCHEN

☐ pantry neat and orderly
☐ sink free of stains and grime
☐ appliances in good working order
☐ unexpired warranty and operating instructions available
☐ range, hood, filter, and ventilator free of accumulated grease, odors

CUPBOARDS

☐ free of excess storage
☐ arrangement orderly
☐ hardware operating
☐ surfaces clear

Item to Be Done	Supplies & Equipment Needed	Cost	To Be Done By	Date

BATHROOM #1

Item to Be Done	Supplies & Equipment Needed	Cost	To Be Done By	Date
☐ replace loose or broken tiles				
☐ caulk joints, if necessary				
☐ brush grime from joints				
☐ leaky faucet repaired				
☐ running or noisy water closet repaired				
☐ sink stains removed				
☐ counters cleared				
☐ guest towels out				
☐ shower curtain, bright, fresh				
☐ hardware and fixtures operating, clean at joints				
☐ peeling wallpaper repaired				
☐ soiled walls washed or repainted				
☐ lights operating				
☐ exhaust fan operating				
☐ floor clean				
☐ drawer and cabinet hardware operating				

BATHROOM #2

- [ ] replace loose or broken tiles
- [ ] caulk joints, if necessary
- [ ] brush grime from joints
- [ ] leaky faucet repaired
- [ ] running or noisy water closet repaired
- [ ] sink stains removed
- [ ] counters cleared
- [ ] guest towels out
- [ ] shower curtain, bright, fresh
- [ ] hardware and fixtures operating, clean at joints
- [ ] peeling wallpaper repaired
- [ ] soiled walls washed or repainted
- [ ] lights operating
- [ ] exhaust fan operating
- [ ] floor clean
- [ ] drawer and cabinet hardware operating

Item to Be Done	Supplies & Equipment Needed	Cost	To Be Done By	Date

BEDROOM #1

- ☐ walls free of water stain
- ☐ wallpaper tight to walls
- ☐ walls clean, free of smudges
- ☐ windows freshly washed
- ☐ cracked or broken panes replaced
- ☐ curtains and drapes clean, fresh
- ☐ hardware present and operating
- ☐ window sashes operate freely
- ☐ window sills clean
- ☐ woodwork recently painted, not soiled, scuffed, or marred
- ☐ floor recently waxed
- ☐ carpets clean, tacked down
- ☐ doors and frames clean or recently painted
- ☐ door hardware operates free of squeaks
- ☐ furniture arranged to best show room size

Item to Be Done	Supplies & Equipment Needed	Cost	To Be Done By	Date

BEDROOM #2

- ☐ walls free of water stain
- ☐ wallpaper tight to walls
- ☐ walls clean, free of smudges
- ☐ windows freshly washed
- ☐ cracked or broken panes replaced
- ☐ curtains and drapes clean, fresh
- ☐ hardware present and operating
- ☐ window sashes operate freely
- ☐ window sills clean
- ☐ woodwork recently painted, not soiled, scuffed, or marred
- ☐ floor recently waxed
- ☐ carpets clean, tacked down
- ☐ doors and frames clean or recently painted
- ☐ door hardware operates free of squeaks
- ☐ furniture arranged to best show room size

Item to Be Done	Supplies & Equipment Needed	Cost	To Be Done By	Date

BEDROOM #3

- [ ] walls free of water stain
- [ ] wallpaper tight to walls
- [ ] walls clean, free of smudges
- [ ] windows freshly washed
- [ ] cracked or broken panes replaced
- [ ] hardware present and operating
- [ ] window sashes operate freely
- [ ] window sills clean
- [ ] woodwork recently painted, not soiled, scuffed, or marred
- [ ] floor recently waxed
- [ ] carpets clean, tacked down
- [ ] doors and frames clean or recently painted
- [ ] door hardware operates free of squeaks
- [ ] furniture arranged to best show room size

Item to Be Done	Supplies & Equipment Needed	Cost	To Be Done By	Date

CHECK LIST
HOW TO PREPARE YOUR HOUSE

☐ MAKE A GOOD FIRST IMPRESSION

☐ SPEND YOUR REMODELING MONEY WISELY

☐ SELL YOUR SPACE

☐ PLAN YOUR RECONDITIONING EARLY

☐ REPAIR MAJOR ITEMS

☐ INSPECT THE EXTERIOR

☐ INSPECT THE BASEMENT

☐ INSPECT THE INTERIOR

☐ HIRE HELP TO GET THE JOB DONE

CHAPTER 3

FOR

HOW TO PREPARE

YOUR SELLING AIDS

SALE

BY OWNER

A fter you establish your asking price and prepare your house for showing, you must concentrate on selling. The best house in the world won't sell by itself. It takes selling, and selling is only effective when the salesman has properly prepared his sales aids.

PREPARE YOUR LISTING SHEET

A communication medium commonly used between residential real estate sellers and prospective buyers is what is called the "listing sheet." A listing sheet may take many forms but is normally one page, approximately six inches by nine inches, printed on one or both sides. It often contains a photograph of the house, the address, the asking price, and other pertinent data. When the house is shown, each prospect is given a listing sheet to provide a full description of the house. The listing sheet is also a constant reminder of the house for the prospect and, therefore, becomes an excellent sales aid.

The listing sheet that you prepare will be an important tool in selling your house. The next chapter will explain in detail how the listing sheet can help you market your house. Basically it should be handed out to your neighbors and given to all prospects who are shown through your house. In this chapter you will find out how to produce a listing sheet.

A completed listing sheet is shown on the following page. For your convenience, three blank listing sheets are provided in Appendix 2 for you to remove, complete, and take to your printer as explained below. (The extra copies have been provided for typing errors or changes you may make.) The process of preparing a listing sheet has been greatly simplified so that you will be able to prepare this valuable sales aid with a minimum of effort. To prepare your listing sheet:

1. Gather your data from: a listing sheet you might have kept when you bought your house; your builder's advertising brochures; the plot plan; or survey, tax and utility bills. These information sources can be convenient references for filling in your listing sheet.
2. Survey your house for the details required and complete a blank listing sheet in pencil.
3. Double check all the items you have recorded, and fill in the blanks. Typing is preferred, but if you can't get it typed then print neatly.
4. Photograph your house and select the best of the prints. Attach the print to the upper portion of the typed listing form.
5. Take the listing form with the attached photo to a local instant printing center and have 150-200 copies printed.

Each item on the listing sheet is explained below so that you will be able to complete the form with no difficulty. The upper portion of the listing sheet is for the photograph of your house. The center portion to the right of the heading ''For Sale By

FOR SALE BY OWNER	**OWNER** R. L. Stone	GRACIOUS COLONIAL
	RES. PHONE 314-968-2551	Completely refurbished. New heating and central air. New kitchen appliances.
	BUS. PHONE 314-271-6160	

1256 Lake Avenue	Pine Grove	7	4	2½	$175,000
ADDRESS	**COMMUNITY**	**ROOMS**	**BDRMS**	**BATH**	**PRICE**

STYLE	Colonial	**PATIO**	New with Gas Grill
CONSTRUCTION	Brick and Frame	**FIREPLACE**	Liv Rm/Rathsler
AGE	Approx. 35 yrs	**CARPETS**	2 yrs. old
LOT SIZE	191 x 60	**DRAPES**	Living Room
SQ. FT.	2700	**HEAT**	Gas Forced Air
LIVING RM.	22 x 13	**AIR COND.**	Central
DINING RM.	13 x 10	**DISHWASHER**	New Kitchenaid
FAMILY RM.	—	**DISPOSAL**	New Incinerator
BEDROOM 1	18 x 16 Master	**STOVE**	New self-clean GE
BEDROOM 2	18 x 14	**CITY WATER**	Yes
BEDROOM 3	14 x 12	**SEWER**	Yes
BEDROOM 4	11 x 10	**PROPERTY TAX**	$2,400 annually
BEDROOM 5	—	**SCHOOL: ELEM.**	Pine Grove
KITCHEN	13 x 12	**J.H.S.**	Wellington
BREAKFAST RM.	15 x 8	**H.S.**	Parkdale
BASEMENT	Rathskeller	**CATH.**	St. Agnes
GARAGE	2 car attached		Heated porch
CLOSETS	7 plus built-ins		Enclosed porch
			New Driveway

Owner'' is provided for entering your name, residence phone, and business phone. If you do not wish prospective buyers to contact you at work, leave the business phone space blank.

The blank section to the right of the owner's name and phone numbers is designed to be used as advertising space. In this space you insert promotional excerpts from the ad that you will place in your local newspaper. Preparation of the ad will be discussed later in this chapter. There is no need in this advertising space to repeat any of the items that are described in the lower portion of the listing sheet unless they are outstanding features of your house.

It is in this space that you should specifically state the positive features of your house that may not be apparent from reading the lower portion of the listing sheet. Examples of statements that might have appeal to prospective buyers are shown below.

WOODED LOT	SECLUDED RANCH
Magnificent Colonial with numerous oaks. Located in cul de sac. Ideal family house with fenced backyard.	Away from the noise of the city and highway, parklike setting. Three acres of trees.

The detail items that make up the lower portion of the listing sheet are explained below:

ADDRESS	Your home address
COMMUNITY	Indicate whether you live in the city or a suburb, e.g., Chicago or a suburb such as Hinsdale, Oak Park, Western Springs

ROOMS	Total number of rooms not including baths, halls, closets, porches, or garage
BEDROOMS	Number of bedrooms
BATH	Number of baths
PRICE	Asking price as discussed in Chapter 1
STYLE	Ranch, split-level, bungalow, English, French château, contemporary, Colonial, Cape Cod, New England, Western Ranch, traditional, New Orleans French, Williamsburg, provincial, Dutch Colonial, cottage
CONSTRUCTION	Frame, brick, stucco, stone, redwood, cedar, brick veneer, aluminum siding, brick and frame
AGE	Age of house; if you are uncertain, indicate by saying "approximate age"
LOT SIZE	Lot size such as 190' x 70' or approx. ½ acre, approx. ⅓ acre (one acre equals 43,560 sq. ft.)
SQUARE FEET	Square footage of living space not including garage, attic, or basement unless the basement has living space such as a family room or playroom
LIVING ROOM	Room dimensions such as 20' x 15'
DINING ROOM	Same as above
FAMILY ROOM	Same as above
BEDROOM NO. 1	Same as above

BEDROOM No. 2	Same as above
BEDROOM No. 3	Same as above
BEDROOM No. 4	Same as above
BEDROOM No. 5	Same as above
KITCHEN	Same as above
BREAKFAST ROOM	Same as above
BASEMENT	Room dimensions, description of finished space—rathskeller, laundry room, playroom
GARAGE	Attached one-car, two-car
CLOSETS	9 closets, ample closet space, large walk-in closets
PATIO	Dimensions such as 20′ x 30′, large brick, flagstone, poured concrete, secluded, with gas grill, screened, overlooking lake
FIREPLACE	Brick, Franklin stove, stone, working, in den, in living room
CARPETS	Wall-to-wall, not included, living room, dining room, new, throughout, some, no, fully
DRAPES	Similar to carpets above
HEAT	Electric, gas, oil, radiant heat, forced air, radiant baseboard, hot water
AIR CONDITIONING	Central, five window units, none, zone central, five-ton central
DISHWASHER	Built-in, G.E., brand-new
DISPOSAL	Yes or no; incinerator
STOVE	Built-in, not included, gas, electric, self-cleaning, G.E., brand-new

CITY WATER	Yes, or well. If well, expect some prospects to ask questions about flowage and sanitation
SEWER	Yes, septic tank, none
PROPERTY TAX	Annual property tax from your latest property tax statement
SCHOOL	Name the elementary, junior high, and high school. (Use the blank space for parochial or other schools.)

The blank spaces on the bottom of the listing sheet can be used to indicate other features of the house which might be appealing to a prospect: attic fan, TV antenna, or swimming pool.

PHOTOGRAPH YOUR HOUSE

It is preferable to use a camera that will provide you with a 3½″ x 5″ black-and-white glossy print. The Kodak Pocket Instamatic and all 35 mm cameras take 3½″ x 5″ prints. You can use square 3″ x 3″ prints but they will not fill the space on the listing sheet as well as 3½″ x 5″. You do not need a special camera, an inexpensive camera will be fine. Take one roll of twelve shots from various angles. If you fail to get a good print, take another roll. Guided by the mistakes made in your first roll, you will undoubtedly get at least one good shot of the house. The total cost of one roll of black-and-white film including the developing should be approximately $5.25. The processing time should only be two or three days. Don't try to economize by taking only one or two shots. Film and developing costs are minimal considering the dollars at stake in selling your house.

In each photo, attempt to include the entire house and as much of the landscaping and trees as possible. Try to get an angle view to show the depth of the house and lot. Wait for a bright and sunny day so the tree shadows convey the warmth of your house. Be certain the area you are photographing is free from signs, cars, ladders, or other equipment that would take the prospect's attention away from your house and yard. Make certain the lawn is freshly cut and trimmed and all visible exterior repairs have been completed before you take these photos. Remember, what the buyer sees is what the buyer thinks he gets!

Taking a good photo is not a difficult task. The photo on the same listing sheet was taken with a Kodak Pocket Instamatic 20. The photographer was inexperienced but look at the beautiful results.

PRINT YOUR LISTING SHEET

Attach the best print to the upper portion of the typed listing sheet and locate a nearby instant printing center (under "Printing" in the Yellow Pages). For approximately $20–$25 the printer will reproduce 150 to 200 copies. For best effect, the printer should prepare a metal plate to get a "half-tone" of your photo. The cost can be cut in half without the metal plate, but the quality of reproduction of your photo may be poor. Remember, this is one of your best selling aids. Most printers should perform this work in about two days. (Ask the printer to trim the white border from your picture and center it in the upper portion of your listing sheet.)

PREPARE YOUR FACT SHEET

In addition to the listing sheet, which provides your prospects with the major characteristics of your house, you must have additional information available when a prospect has been shown your house and then indicates that he desires more information to help him make a decision. A "fact sheet" has been designed for this purpose. The fact sheet will not be used in the advertisement of your house. It contains information that will be required only when a prospect has visited your house and has a sincere interest in obtaining further information. The fact sheet is the same size and basic format as the listing sheet. It can be easily stapled to the listing sheet so that interested prospects will have a complete package of information.

A completed fact sheet is shown on the following page. For your convenience, three blank fact sheets are provided in Appendix 2 for you to remove, complete, and have copied as explained below. (The extra copies are provided for typing errors or changes you might make.)

Your completed fact sheet can be copied on any copying machine or taken to your instant printing center with your listing sheet. It will be cheaper to run the copies on a copying machine and cut them to the 6" x 9" size to match the listing sheet. You will probably require at least twenty-five copies of the fact sheet.

After a prospect has "fallen in love" with the features of your house he eventually turns his attention to the expense of owning your house. A commonly used term in residential real estate is "PITI," which refers to the monthly payment for principal, interest, taxes, and insurance. Frequently, all of these expenses are combined into one payment that is made to the mortgage company and is often considered one expense.

The buyer will contact his banker or savings and loan officer to calculate the monthly principal and interest payments or you may assist him. (See Chapter 6 on financing.) He will then request information on the taxes and insurance.

The first item to record under expenses on the fact sheet is your monthly expense for real property taxes. You have indicated the annual property taxes on your listing sheet. Divide this figure by 12 to arrive at the monthly tax expense. Frequently there are real property taxes for both state and city. Include both under property tax expenses. The taxes you should record are for real estate (not personal) property. Do not include any personal property taxes, which are based on the value of automobiles, furniture, and other personal property. Have copies of your latest real property tax bill handy. The buyer's real property tax will be about the same as yours but his personal property tax may be quite different.

FOR SALE
BY OWNER

OWNER	R. L. Stone
ADDRESS	1256 Lake Avenue
RES. PHONE	(314) 968-2551
BUS. PHONE	(314) 271-6160

EXPENSES

	$ Per Month
Property Taxes	$200
Electric	$60
Gas	$50
Water	$18
Sewer	$4
Refuse Collection	$4
Subdivision Association	$20

ITEMS INCLUDED WITH HOUSE

Wall-to-wall carpet: Living Room, Dining Room, Hall, and Stairs
Drapes: Living Room
Venetian Blinds
Storm Windows
Screens
TV Antenna in Attic

Some prospects may also want to review the taxes that you have paid, not only for last year but also for the two years prior, in order to determine the amount of recent tax increases. Rapid property tax increases have not been uncommon in many parts of the country and are a matter of concern to buyers. Your own review of the trends of your property taxes will help you discuss this issue frankly with the prospects who inquire.

Often a house is assessed at a certain fraction of its market value. By referring to this assessed value the prospective buyer may make a calculation that he feels provides him with a "fair market value." Don't let him put this one over on you. There is no reason to believe that the value placed on your house by the tax assessor has any relationship to its current market value. The assessment may have been made several years ago. The assessor was probably working with tax valuation, and not with the prospect of selling your house in the open marketplace.

Another important item under expenses is the monthly fire and extended coverage, or "homeowners," insurance premium that you are paying for coverage on your house. You should have your policy handy. You should know the name, address, and telephone number of your agent, the specific type of coverage, the expiration date and the monthly cost.

Most insurance companies now issue a "package" policy, which includes coverage for your personal articles such as jewelry, cameras, and collectors' items. The premiums reflect extra coverages and make it impossible to transfer the policy to your buyer. However, unless you have an unusual number of separately scheduled items in your policy, the premiums should still be indicative of a buyer's insurance expense. Having this information available will help the prospect make an informed estimate of his monthly expenses. He is thereby one step closer to knowing if he can make a deal with you.

In addition to the principal, interest, taxes, and insurance the prospect will be interested in your monthly operating expenses such as electric, gas, water, sewer, and refuse collection. He may be interested in the average winter heating bill and the average summer air-conditioning bill. You will have difficulty satisfying a curious prospect if you only have one bill from last month available. It is best to locate the bills for the last twelve months. Call your utility company if you are unable to find your bills and request that they provide you with this information. After you have collected these bills enter the monthly expense on an "operating expense sheet." A completed operating expense sheet is shown on the following page. For your convenience, three blank copies are provided in Appendix 2.

Calculate the twelve-month average of these expenses and enter the average on your fact sheet. Have this monthly detail and your bills available in case the buyer requests it.

The next section to be completed on the fact sheet is a listing of those items that are included in the selling price of your house. Although the real estate custom includes "fixtures" in the sale of the house, there is generally confusion over the definition of "fixtures" and it is wise to spell out carefully each item that you intend to sell with your house. (See Chapter 7.)

Certain items that are not easily "movable" and are tailor-made for your house should be included in your price and listed on your fact sheet as "items included with house":

wall-to-wall carpeting	screens
storm windows	water softener
lighting fixtures	sump pump
TV antenna	central air conditioner
awnings	

In many instances these "movable" items can be selling points when you are trying to market your house. Wall-to-wall carpeting, storm windows, and other items can be expensive and are sometimes a blessing in disguise when the prospect realizes that he will not have to incur these costs. You may also have an attractive chandelier in your dining room that enhances the beauty of the room. This can be a good selling feature when showing your house and should be listed on your fact sheet. There are other items that are "movable" but that you may want to sell with your house. Don't list these items on the "fact sheet" but have a separate list available and fix a price for each item in your mind, in the event the prospect is interested:

FOR SALE BY OWNER

OWNER	R. L. Stone
ADDRESS	1256 Lake Avenue
RES. PHONE	(314) 968-2551
BUS. PHONE	(314) 271-6160

Month	Elec.	Gas	Water	Sewer	Refuse	
Mar.	$40.00	$66.38	$17.00	$4.00	$4.00	
Apr.	40.94	52.60	16.50	4.00	4.00	
May	42.30	44.56	20.50	4.00	4.00	
June	70.00	36.40	22.00	4.00	4.00	
July	94.38	35.00	24.96	4.00	4.00	
Aug.	89.30	35.00	25.04	4.00	4.00	
Sept.	80.60	37.40	18.00	4.00	4.00	
Oct.	61.96	37.24	18.00	4.00	4.00	
Nov.	49.22	47.20	14.00	4.00	4.00	
Dec.	50.80	67.08	14.00	4.00	4.00	
Jan.	51.50	68.50	13.20	4.00	4.00	
Feb.	49.00	72.64	12.80	4.00	4.00	
Total	720.00	600.00	216.00	48.00	48.00	
Avg. Mo.	60.00	50.00	18.00	4.00	4.00	

refrigerator   barbecue grill
humidifier   workbench
window air conditioner   washing machine
birdbath   children's swing set
window fan   dryer
lawn mower   fireplace equipment

Drapes and curtains may fall into either category. If they were custom-made for an unusual size window you might consider them a part of the house and include them in your price. If they are easily "movable" you might price them separately.

Additional space is provided at the bottom of the fact sheet for other items that you may want to bring to the attention of the prospect. If you have arranged with your mortgage company to allow a qualified buyer to assume your mortgage, indicate so in this section of the fact sheet. Note the name and address of the mortgage company, the balance remaining, the interest rate, the monthly principal and interest payments, and the term of the mortgage. Be prepared to help the prospect understand the financing aspects of purchasing your house. This can be a critical selling tool and help close the deal. (See Chapter 6.)

You can also mention in this blank section of the fact sheet any specific easements that exist on your property or easements you have on neighboring property.

If there are special locational features that may be of specific interest to the prospect, indicate them in this section. If you are twenty minutes from downtown, within two miles of a major shopping center, or close to a major recreational facility, mention this as an additional selling feature.

If you desire, this section can be left blank and used by the prospect to record notes while he is viewing your house. You can type in the heading "Buyer's Notes" so he knows this space is for his use.

GATHER ADDITIONAL DATA

In addition to the information you record on the listing sheet and fact sheet, there is certain other information that is readily available that could be very helpful in closing your sale.

Have a map of your city available. With a felt pen circle the location of your house, the elementary school, high school, junior high, parks, and major shopping areas. Excellent one-page maps of your city can usually be obtained at a car-rental counter at the airport. This selling aid can be extremely helpful to out-of-town prospects.

Also call your chamber of commerce. They will provide you with key statistics on your city and bring you up-to-date on cultural and civic activities that may be of interest to your prospect.

DESIGN YOUR ADVERTISING PROGRAM

Advertising is nothing more than a form of communication that you must establish between yourself and your prospect. To be an effective communicator you must understand the basic elements of your advertising media. You are well aware of the many methods of advertising such as TV, radio, newspaper, and direct mail. Each method has its inherent advantages and disadvantages and each is particularly suited to reach a specific type of audience with a specific product. The most effective method for advertising residential real estate is the classified section of your local newspaper. It is here that you will concentrate the bulk of your advertising dollars to find your buyer.

Open the pages of the classified advertising section of your local newspaper and locate the section on residential real estate. You have competition! But there are also prospects! There will be hundreds and possibly thousands of prospects scanning the classfied advertising section and it will be your task to properly motivate qualified prospects to seek further information regarding your house.

Let's get a better understanding of how to motivate prospects. All basic human needs can be classified in one of four general categories: security, affection, prestige, and self-expression. If you take a minute to concentrate on these categories you will conclude that the purchase of a home plays an important role in fulfilling each of these needs.

Fear of the ever-increasing crime rate is often a motivating factor in selecting a home and satisfies the basic human need for *security*.

Providing one's family with a "Home Sweet Home" rather than just a roof over their heads goes a long way toward satisfying man's need for *affection*.

Our society has created an atmosphere where most men and women are very conscious of their need for social approval. What is more basic in fulfilling this *prestige* need than the approval that people look for from their relatives and friends when they visit their house?

The highest order of the human need is *self-expression*. Gardening and home decorating have become important outlets for fulfilling man's need for self-expression amidst the background of increasing mechanization.

Although the classified newspaper ad you place may not be able to appeal to all of the human needs discussed, you should view your house as a commodity that has the potential of satisfying some of these needs. Find out what needs your house best fulfills and construct the appeal in your ad accordingly. Write your ad so that it hits the buyer hard. Relate these needs to the context of your ad. Sample "headlines" that correspond to the basic human needs are listed below:

Need	*Headline*
Security	SECLUDED NEIGHBORHOOD
	TRAFFIC-FREE
	PRIVACY
Affection	PLACE FOR TOTS
	FOR THE ACTIVE FAMILY
	KIDS AND CLOVER
Prestige	ESCAPE FROM THE ORDINARY
	LUXURY COLONIAL
	JET-AGE LIVING
Self-Expression	MODERN ELEGANCE
	NEWLY RENOVATED
	DECORATOR'S DELIGHT

The headlines above are only one way of expressing the "need" concept in your ads. The same concept should be used in constructing your appeal message in the body of the ad.

IDENTIFY YOUR AUDIENCE

You have only one objective in preparing your classified ad. Your objective must be to motivate a qualified prospect to be so interested in the description of your house that he will contact you to obtain further information or stop by to visit your house. Once the contact has been made and he has had an opportunity to view your house, you will be able to make use of your other selling techniques to close the sale.

Uppermost in your mind must be the type of individual or family that is most likely to purchase your house. You must identify your audience and find a way to appeal to his needs. You should know the families living in your neighborhood and have a basic understanding of their income levels and socio-logical and ethnic characteristics. If you live in a neighborhood of young couples with small children, you will be appealing to a totally different audience than if you live in a neighborhood characterized by couples whose children have reached college age. Picture the prospect that you want to reach and then construct your ad as if you were talking directly to your prospect.

Take special notice of those features of your house that will appeal to the audience that you have selected. Consider the fenced backyard for children, proximity to a shopping center for a retired couple, or proximity to a junior college for a young married couple.

When you contact your local newspaper you will be asked the section of the residential classified ads in which you want your ad to appear. Many newspapers classify the ads by sections of the city. You will undoubtedly be listed under the section in which your house is located: North, Southwest, or under a particular suburb. It may not be adequate to list only your street address, depending on your location. Many prospects and especially out-of-town prospects may not be familiar with your street or with the general characteristics of your location. If a characteristic forms a good selling point, try to include it in your ad:

Located two blocks from Lake Michigan
Within walking distance of Radner High
One mile from the Colonial Shopping Center

Two miles from Chicago Northwestern train
Across the street from Miller's Park
Two blocks from Stanford University

If you have moved out of your house (and fear theft or vandalism) or if you do not want strangers stopping, list the street name and number but show the last two digits of the street number as "xx." For example, 1254 Foxboro Road would be listed as 12xx Foxboro Road.

The price of the house is also essential in limiting your appeal to qualified buyers. An appealing ad without a price may draw twenty-five people to your open house and only a handful might be financially capable of purchasing the house. You will save yourself a great deal of time and effort if you indicate the asking price in your ad. State the exact asking price and don't beat around the bush by saying between $140,000 and $150,000 or approximately $150,000.

It is also important to clearly state the basic physical characteristics of the house, especially the number of bedrooms and baths. Other selling features such as family room, den, swimming pool, formal dining room, fireplace, patio, tennis courts and finished basement will help direct your appeal to the right audience.

Don't fail to mention that the style of your house is Colonial, English half-timber or Spanish-style ranch. Most prospects have already determined the style of house that they prefer.

SELECT A HEADLINE

Before you motivate your audience, you must first attract their attention. There are various advertising "layout" techniques such as bold type and heavy bordering. Look to your local newspaper for these "layout" ideas to attract attention by physically structuring your ad. It may cost a little extra to use one of these techniques but if it attracts the eye of a prospect it will have been well worthwhile.

Many prospects will immediately be attracted to your ad if you indicate "By Owner." Prospects generally have a feeling that they will get a better deal if they have the opportunity to bargain directly with the owner rather than a real estate broker. Some prospects feel that it might be a good location and a good house if the owner has the confidence to market the house himself rather than list with a real estate broker. Your ad should *always* include "By Owner."

Below "By Owner" you should use a "headline" to draw attention to your ad. In constructing your headline don't be corny and don't exaggerate. There is nothing wrong, however, with a little sex appeal. The American public is accustomed to a degree of creativity and showmanship in advertising. Select the most appealing feature of your house and work this into your headline. Look over the headlines below that were selected from various residential classified ads throughout the country:

Magnificent	Forest setting
Privacy	Prestige Area
Security	Fresh & Sparkling
Spread Out	Magnificent View
Home of the Month	Entertain
Today's Best	Plush
A Bright Future	Rustic Contemporary
Incredible Find	Elegant
Special & Spacious	Rare Opportunity
Holiday House	Move-in Condition
Gracious Colonial	Place for Tots
Near Everything	Love a Fireplace?

Bold but Elegant
Country Living
Don't Delay
Looking for Privacy?
You'll be Surprised
Why Pay Rent
Traffic-Free
Abide in Luxury
Not Very Often
Walk to Shopping
Charming Landscape
Fine Old Trees
A Charmer
Just Perfect
Cathedral Ceilings
Circular Drive
Country Air
Room to Run
The Active Family
Attention!!!
Charming White Brick
Ideal for Couple
Invest in the Future
Trees
Clean and Compact
Best Value Home
Outstanding
New Listing
Country Living
Modern Elegance
Great Area
Horse Lovers
You'll Fall in Love
Call to See This

Park-like Setting
Starter Home
You'll Like It
Unusual, Exciting
Luxury Colonial
Outstanding Value
Delightful
Want to Be Alone?
Charm
Rare Bargain
Search no More
Quiet Neighborhood
Old World Charm
Picturesque Setting
Rolling Hills
Peace and Quiet
Better than New
A Gracious Home
Cozy Fireplace
What a Way to Live
Lovely Ranch
Must Sell
Excellent Location
Need Four Bedrooms?
Don't Miss This
This Is a Beauty
Must Be Sold
Excellent Condition
The Best Buy
All Brick
Lots of Land
How Can You Resist?
Newly Decorated
Take Time to Live

Kids and Clover	A Distinguished Home
Want Spaciousness?	This Is It!
Common Ground	Executive Home
Prestige Area	Need More Room
Move Right In	A Real Buy
Move in and Relax	Whispering Trees
Jet Age Living	Story Book House

DON'T USE ABBREVIATIONS

A word of caution about abbreviations. Many real estate ads contain abbreviations for practically every conceivable word. It would be simple enough to construct an ad as follows:

BEAUT COL 4 BDRMS

2 BATH, LG DIN RM

ATT 1 CAR GAR

NR SHP CNTR

A real estate agent would have no difficulty deciphering what you have listed in your ad and you will save a few dollars by limiting the number of lines in your ad. But the ad is cold and unimaginative. It completely fails to appeal to the basic human needs which were described earlier. You may have captured the reader's attention with your headline but lost him with your abbreviations. Your ad should be attractive, clear, and concise, not dull and difficult to read.

SELECT EFFECTIVE DESCRIPTIVE WORDS

There are numerous descriptive words that can be helpful in creating your ad. Only you can supply the appropriate words to describe the attractive features of your house. Listed below are some words and phrases that may be of some assistance:

Attractive	Modernized
Updated	Spacious
Charming	Meticulously maintained
Highly desirable	Tastefully updated
Preserved	Beautiful
Unique	Exquisite
Functional	Contemporary
Distinguished	Impressive
Secluded	Rare
Exclusive	Truly Luxurious
Livable floor plan	Generous yard
Separate dining room	Contoured patio
Extensively remodeled	Rustic setting

DEMAND ACTION

The final words in your ad should be an appeal for the reader to take action. Don't get his attention with a headline, heighten his interest in the body of the ad, and then leave him hanging. If you bring him this far, demand he take action.

Close with action-oriented phrases:

Call 763-4184 or 767-5918
Stop by—Sunday 2-4 or call 721-6484
Call for an appointment 661-4132
Don't hesitate, call now 473-8154

WRITE YOUR AD

You have all the tools available to select a headline, appeal to your prospect's needs in the body of your ad, and demand action. Now write several ads and select the best. Sleep on your selection one night and rewrite it. You can usually improve on your work by taking a fresh view the next day. Several sample ads are shown on this page to assist you in writing your ad.

BY OWNER

SPANISH-LOVERS—ATTENTION
22 Baylor Ct. This Spanish-style ranch will surely capture your heart! Beautiful corner lot, 3 bedrooms, 2 baths, separate dining room, family room with brick fireplace, central air, basement, garage, many extras - even a stream with a big old tree. $160,000. Call 228-8620

BY OWNER

OLD WORLD CHARM
Oldham County, 21 Houston Lane. Four acres. Lovely frame cottage with a family room, kitchen combination with wood-burning brick fireplace, full bath with tub and shower, 2 bedrooms, 2 car garage. Priced for immediate sale at $107,000. Call 425-6151 for an appointment.

BY OWNER

IT WILL LEAVE YOU BREATHLESS
31xx Creekside Drive. A really luxurious 4 bedroom, 2½ bath, colonial, with wall-to-wall carpeting, 2 car garage, basement, central air conditioning, 1st floor family room with fireplace, lovely convenient kitchen with planning desk for Mother. $117,000. Call 487-5418

BY OWNER

CONVENIENT LOCATION
Cherokee Garden Area, 613 Crestwood Drive. Perfect home for someone wanting to be close-in and yet have privacy. Dead-end street, 3 bedrooms, 2½ baths plus toilet in basement. Library and living room have fireplaces, large screened porch. Home is 13 years old. Fenced backyard for children. $133,000. Call now - 462-5178

PREPARE YOUR SIGN

An important medium of your advertising program is the sign that you will place in your front yard. Properly painted and placed it will make all of your neighbors aware of your desire to sell. It will also appeal to people driving through your neighborhood who may have missed your newspaper ad.

Unless you are artistic by nature it is advisable to call a professional sign company. Signs vary in size but standard "For Sale" signs are either 21" high by 27" wide or 24" high by 36" wide. The larger sign is preferable, especially if placement will be some distance from the street. The smaller sign, painted any color on white background (both sides), should be around $35.00 and the larger sign around $40.00. This rate will obviously vary from city to city.

Most sign companies will be able to prepare your sign within two days of the time you place the order. Unless you live on a one-way street it is essential that you have both sides painted. Place the sign at a right angle to your house so that it can be read by prospects passing on either side of the street. Large, bold black or red lettering on white background will attract the attention of passersby.

Your sign should definitely be painted "For Sale by Owner." Even though there is no real estate broker's name on the sign it may not be apparent to prospects that this house is being offered "By Owner." It is a selling point in your favor that the potential buyer knows that it is to be sold "By Owner." Beneath "For Sale by Owner" indicate "for appointment call." Below this line paint your telephone number. If you have an alternate phone number for your office indicate both phone numbers. Make certain that the printing is large enough to read from the street so that prospects do not have to leave their automobiles to read your telephone number.

If you have decided to have an open house, purchase a small "Open" sign that can be attached to the larger "For Sale by Owner" sign. If you live in a neighborhood where you can place a sign at the end of your block to draw traffic, consider purchasing a second sign to be used on the open-house days.

A sign can be an important sales aid. In St. Paul, Minnesota, one "For Sale by Owner" sign sold over a dozen houses in one neighborhood. The sign was quite large, beautifully painted and indicated "For Sale by Owner." Due to repeated success, each new seller simply painted his telephone number on the sign, stuck the sign in his front yard, and waited for the results.

CHECK LIST
HOW TO PREPARE YOUR SELLING AIDS

☐ PREPARE YOUR LISTING SHEET

☐ PHOTOGRAPH YOUR HOUSE

☐ PRINT YOUR LISTING SHEET

☐ PREPARE YOUR FACT SHEET

☐ GATHER ADDITIONAL DATA

☐ DESIGN YOUR ADVERTISING PROGRAM

☐ IDENTIFY YOUR AUDIENCE

☐ SELECT A HEADLINE

☐ DON'T USE ABBREVIATIONS

☐ SELECT EFFECTIVE DESCRIPTIVE WORDS

☐ DEMAND ACTION

☐ WRITE YOUR AD

☐ PREPARE YOUR SIGN

CHAPTER 4

FOR

HOW TO MARKET YOUR HOUSE

SALE

BY OWNER

You have prepared all the necessary selling aids. Your next step is to go to market. During this phase of selling your house you must concentrate all of your efforts, pursuing every possible avenue to the marketplace. One marketing approach will not be sufficient. Don't expect to hand out one listing sheet or place one newspaper ad and find an immediate buyer. Remember, knowledge of your "product," perseverance, and patience will produce the desired results . . . a buyer and seller who are both totally satisfied!

DISTRIBUTE YOUR LISTING SHEETS

If you have lived in your house for any length of time, you know many of your neighbors and will probably be able to identify those who have a "nose for news." These individuals can be an important part of your sales program.

Invite these "newscasters," and as many other neighbors as you know, over to your house for coffee. Take them on a tour. Sell them on the important features of the house. Don't forget to give each of them several listing sheets to distribute to their friends. Your neighbors will be your most active supporters, since they are already sold on living in your neighborhood. It is also to their own advantage to make certain that their new neighbors (who purchase the house from you) are the type of people they want living on their block.

In addition to having an "open house" for your neighbors, consider stuffing the mailboxes in your neighborhood with listing sheets. Attach a short note to the listing sheets stating that your house is for sale. Express the hope that, as neighbors, they would help. Ask them to contact you if they have any questions or wish to see the house. Briefly mention why you are moving, so they understand why you are leaving their neighborhood. Obviously, you shouldn't tell them that you are moving to a better neighborhood. Either use the correct reason for the move, "transferred out-of-town," or dream up one that will not offend them.

Your church group may be a logical place to circulate listing sheets. Families usually ask their close friends if they know of houses for sale in their area. Notify your pastor or rabbi of your intention to sell, and give him several listing sheets.

If there is a university close by, contact the campus housing department and ask them to put a record of your house on file and to place your listing sheet on the bulletin board. You should be certain a few faculty members living in your neighborhood have a listing sheet, as their fellow professors may be interested in your house.

If there is a large corporation in your area, make an appointment to see the personnel director. He may know of people being transferred from out-of-town who would like to locate in your neighborhood. He will keep a record of your house on file and also may put your listing sheet on the company bulletin board.

Find the center of activity in your neighborhood. It may be

the beauty parlor or drugstore. Place your listing sheet on the bulletin board and give several copies to the proprietor.

The listing sheet will also aid you in responding to telephone inquiries that originate from your newspaper ads. When you receive phone calls regarding your ad, take the name and address of the caller and tell him you will drop a listing sheet in the mail. The local mail will be received the following day and your prospect will have a much better indication of the specifications of your house.

Some communities have agencies that work in conjunction with the chamber of commerce to promote the local area. Often out-of-town families will contact one of these agencies when they are looking for local housing. Locate this agency in your community and drop off several listing sheets.

CHECK NEWSPAPER CIRCULATION

By following the guidelines in Chapter 3 you have prepared a newspaper ad that will appeal to prospective buyers. Now you must find the advertising space that provides the best return on your advertising dollar. Check the circulation of each local newspaper, including suburban newspapers. Although it is obviously best to reach as large an audience as possible, it is not always economically feasible. If there are two city newspapers and one suburban newspaper, it may be too costly to advertise in all three. Your house may remain on the market for several weeks and the cumulative cost of advertising may be staggering. You must be selective.

If your advertising budget requires that you limit your ads to one newspaper, compare the circulation with the rate schedule to determine the readership per advertising dollar.

Assume newspaper A has a Sunday circulation of 2,000,000 and your ad costs $30 per Sunday . . . newspaper B has a Sunday circulation of 1,500,000 and your ad costs $20 per Sunday . . . newspaper A reaches 167,000 readers per advertising dollar (2,000,000 readers divided by $30). Newspaper B reaches 175,000 readers per advertising dollar (1,500,000 divided by $20). Although newspaper A has the larger circulation, the cost to reach each reader is higher. If the cost differential between newspapers is insignificant, it may be better to spend a little more to get wider circulation.

Don't select a newspaper based on cost analysis alone. Review the real estate ads in each newspaper. Some newspapers are more popular in some areas of a city than in others. The number of ads for houses selling in your area will give some indication of the readership you can expect.

OBTAIN ADVERTISING RATES

After determining the circulation of both the weekday and Sunday editions, ask each newspaper's classified representative to mail you the advertising rate card for classified ads. Most rate cards will show two types of discounts. One will be based on the number of lines and the other on the number of consecutive advertising days. Most discounts are available only for consecutive days of advertising and are not available for consecutive Sundays.

Advertising rates will vary from city to city depending on circulation. Per-line cost in medium-size cities might range from $1.50 to $5.00. Per-line cost in larger cities might range from $4.00 to $8.00. These costs will then be discounted based on the number of lines and the number of consecutive advertising days.

The cost might increase from $1.50 per line to $2.00 per

line for the Sunday edition. Sunday circulation is wider than weekdays and readership in the classified section is usually substantially greater.

Suburban newspaper rates are generally less expensive. This can be an excellent medium for selling your house. Check the suburban rates and analyze the number of real estate ads in your area.

CALCULATE YOUR ADVERTISING COSTS

One line of standard-size classified-ad type, one column wide, will contain about five words or thirty letters and spaces. In the trade this is called an "agate" line. Enlarge the type size and obviously the number of words is reduced. If you request, the newspaper will send you the type sizes available.

The body of your ad should be printed in agate type. "By Owner" and your headline should be "10 point" capitals, which takes the same space as two agate lines. "By Owner" and your headline should be two agate lines to draw attention to your ad. A blank line should be left between "By Owner" and your headline. The body of your ad may start directly below the headline. You should be able to adequately describe your house in the body of the ad with eight to ten lines. Your total space, including "By Owner" and your headline may vary between twelve and fifteen lines. This space will provide you with excellent exposure in the classified section.

Prepare the body of your ad and count the number of words at five words to the line. Add two lines for "By Owner," one line for a space between "By Owner" and the headline, and two lines for the headline. Refer to the rate cards or contact the classified representative. Calculate the cost of placing this ad in the classified section for a varying number of days. This will give you a preliminary look at your newspaper advertising costs.

It is unlikely that you will be able to sell your house with one ad. Unless, of course, you have priced your house well below the market, or there is a very unusual demand factor in your community. Plan to have some form of continued advertising campaign.

Based on the economics of selling your house, you can reduce your advertising expense by cutting the body of the ad back to five or six lines and dropping the headline. To have any appeal, a minimum ad would have two lines of "By Owner" followed immediately by a body of approximately five lines. This minimum cost for one Sunday might range anywhere from $10 to $30 depending on the circulation of the newspaper. But don't try to start cutting costs until you have analyzed the economics.

Let's assume there are two local newspapers in your city. Both newspapers charge $5.00 per line for a Sunday ad and $2 per line for a weekday ad. If you run a ten-line ad in one newspaper for three consecutive Sundays, and the two full weeks between these three Sundays, it will cost $20 per weekday and $50 per Sunday; $20 per weekday for 12 weekdays equals $240; $50 per Sunday for three Sundays equals $150. Your total cost is $390. (You will probably get a discount of 5 to 10 percent for running fifteen consecutive days.) If you run a minimum seven-line ad under the same conditions your total cost is $273.

If you extend the above fifteen-line ad program to cover both newspapers your total cost is $780. The seven-line ad cost is $546. The above calculations illustrate the expense involved in newspaper advertising. Remember that the illustration was for only three weeks. Selling your house may take two to five times longer and the costs will increase proportionately.

Review the weekday versus the Sunday classified ads.

You may come to the conclusion that it does not pay to advertise during the week. If there are few real estate ads on weekdays, compared to Sundays, your readership will be low and the effectiveness of your advertising dollar greatly reduced.

In this situation stress Sundays and spend your advertising dollars on ads with more lines and more appeal. A ten-line ad at $2.00 per line for six Sundays costs $120. After six Sundays you should have a fair indication of the response that you will be getting for your house.

Relate your advertising budget to the price of your house. The commission on a $150,000 house at 6 percent is $9,000. The commission on a $130,000 house at 6 percent is $7,800. It is obvious from the commission savings that the seller of the $150,000 house can afford a more elaborate advertising program than the seller of the $130,000 house.

Although the seller of the $150,000 house will save more commission dollars, his advertising costs will tend to be higher than the seller of the $130,000 house. The $150,000 house may have more features and may require more ad lines to describe it than the $130,000 house will. There also may be fewer prospects for the $150,000 house and the seller may have to run his ad for a longer period of time.

Calculate the commission savings you will have available and allocate a portion for advertising. You can expect to spend somewhere between 10 and 20 percent of your commission savings on newspaper advertising. This will vary from community to community and from house to house.

Estimate how long it may take to sell your house and then calculate your advertising costs under various conditions. A good house may sell in six to eight weeks and a difficult house in a poor market may take as long as twelve to sixteen weeks. If you sell your house in six weeks and have run a fifteen-line ad on Sundays at $2.00 per line, you would have spent $180.

If it takes twelve weeks to sell your house you would have spent $360. This may appear expensive, but compare this expense to the commission that you would have paid on your house. Both $180 and $360 appear relatively small when compared to a $7,800 commission on a $130,00 house and a $9,000 commission on a $150,000 house.

PLACE YOUR NEWSPAPER AD

Aim to sell your house as soon as possible because "time is money." There is no way to avoid spending advertising dollars, but you *can* spend your money wisely. Don't attempt to save a few extra dollars in advertising and end up with your house on the market for an inordinate length of time. In the long run it will cost you more to have your house remain on the market than to do your advertising job properly.

Many suburban newspapers allow you to insert a picture of your house above the ad. These newspapers generally have less expensive advertising rates. Call to determine whether or not they will accept a picture and check the rates. There is no question that an attractive picture is "worth a thousand words."

CONDUCT AN OPEN HOUSE

Conducting an open house has both advantages and disadvantages. One advantage is that some people do not like to make appointments and are more comfortable visiting during an open house. A Sunday afternoon "driver" may be driving through your neighborhood. He may stop in at your open house and just might become a "prospect" and eventually a "buyer."

One disadvantage of an open house is the number of "lookers" that enjoy touring houses with no intention of purchasing. These people can be a nuisance and distract the serious prospect who might be visiting your house at the same time. Observe your visitors closely and you will soon be able to spot the "lookers." Beware also of kleptomaniacs or thieves who may pick up pieces of jewelry while you are opening the front door for your next visitor. Avoid this problem by removing everything of value that can be picked up.

PLACE YOUR SIGN

Place your sign in your front yard at right angles to the street so that it can be read by drivers passing in either direction. Be certain that the telephone number can be read from the street and that the sign is not blocked by any trees or parked cars.

If you are having an open house, buy a small "OPEN" sign. During the open house attach the "OPEN" sign to your "For Sale by Owner" sign. Consider placing another "For Sale by Owner" sign with an "OPEN" sign attached at the end of your block to direct traffic to your open house.

TALK IT UP

One of the most effective means of communication is by "word of mouth." Whether you are at work, at a cocktail party, playing tennis, at church, or visiting someone in the hospital, don't fail to mention that you have placed your house on the market. Ask your friends for names of people who might have an interest in your house. The "word" may be passed through three or four people and the fourth person may take an interest . . . this may be your buyer. He may have been unreachable by any other means but by ''word of mouth.''

CHECK LIST
HOW TO MARKET YOUR HOUSE

☐ DISTRIBUTE YOUR LISTING SHEETS

☐ CHECK NEWSPAPER CIRCULATION

☐ OBTAIN ADVERTISING RATES

☐ CALCULATE YOUR ADVERTISING COSTS

☐ PLACE YOUR NEWSPAPER AD

☐ CONDUCT AN OPEN HOUSE

☐ PLACE YOUR SIGN

☐ TALK IT UP

CHAPTER 5

FOR SALE

HOW TO SHOW YOUR HOUSE

BY OWNER

I f you are a salesman or have had prior selling experience, the selling techniques discussed in this chapter will be obvious to you. Even if you have not had direct experience as a salesman, whether you realize it or not, you probably spend a great part of your day selling. You may be a machine-shop foreman, carpenter, lawyer, draftsman, or accountant. If you stop to think about it for a moment, you will realize that a good part of your time *is* involved in selling. You must continually motivate or sell the people who work for you. You must continually motivate or sell your boss (if you want to convince him that you deserve a raise).

Don't start out by telling yourself you can't sell. Think about how much selling you do everyday. You will realize in many respects, you are a salesman.

Certainly no one has a greater stake than you in selling your house. You and your family are the ones most affected by the outcome of the sale. You want the best price in the shortest period of time. There is no doubt that you are highly motivated to sell.

FOLLOW THESE RULES OF GOOD SALESMANSHIP

To be successful in selling your house you must follow these key rules of good salesmanship:

1. Be enthusiastic! Don't be a blah. Be exciting when you talk. For most people, looking for a house is an adventure. The possibility of upgrading their standards is an exhilarating experience and you must both nourish and share this experience with them.
2. Show self-confidence! Put on your Sunday best but don't dress offensively. There is no reason to put on a fancy coat and tie if you don't live in a fancy coat and tie neighborhood. Just be yourself and relax!
3. Look successful! Prospects who would like to move into your neighborhood want to think the people who live there are successful.
4. Always show a positive attitude! Don't let the buyer be negative when he is looking at your house. Appear positive about every aspect of your house.
5. Be cheerful and smile! Make the buyer feel at home. Compliment the buyer on his car, his children, or anything that makes him feel positive toward you and, especially, positive toward your house.

KNOW YOUR TERRITORY

Be prepared to answer any questions. The best attribute of any salesman is "knowing his territory." No one knows your house better than you, but make certain you are prepared.

Your prospect may be interested in the type of trees, bushes, and grass on your property. It will certainly add to the excitement of your sales pitch if you mention "the pin oak that shades the house in the summer," or "the Japanese holly bushes that surround the entrance porch," or "the bluegrass in the backyard." If you are not prepared to discuss these features, take a sample leaf or trimming to your local nursery. They will give you the names of your trees and bushes.

Be prepared to discuss all of your appliances. You may not have paid any attention to your garbage disposal or dishwasher, but your prospect may be interested. Know the brand names and speak enthusiastically about their quality. If there are warranties in effect on any of the appliances, have them available.

If there are any extra items in your house such as a refrigerator, lawn mower, or barbecue pit that you might consider selling with the house, make certain that you have decided on an asking price for each of these items. If the buyer asks, don't hesitate to state your asking price for each item you are willing to sell with the house. Sometimes these "added attractions" provide an incentive to the prospect, and increase his interest.

Be prepared to discuss the local schools, the proximity of major shopping centers, churches in the area, and any other features that may be of interest to your prospect. Make yourself familiar with all of the special features of your neighborhood and community. They may be important considerations to your prospect.

SELL WHEN THE TELEPHONE RINGS

Your first contact with your prospect will probably be on the telephone. A discourteous answer on the telephone could lose the sale. Put a "smile" in your voice when you answer the telephone. Sound happy that the prospect called. Be alive and friendly.

The prospect may say that he is calling about your ad in the paper. Your response should be something like, "Yes, I'm glad you called, would you like me to tell you about the house?" Ask his name so that you can refer to it as you respond. When he asks questions give him prompt and courteous answers. Don't elaborate and *don't* oversell. Ask if he would like to see the house. Try to arrange an appointment. Don't be too pushy.

If you are unable to make an appointment, ask if he would like you to mail a listing sheet. When he receives the listing sheet it may spark enough interest for him to call back for an appointment.

Use the same basic advertising techniques on the telephone that you use in writing your ad. Get his attention. Tell him something exciting. Ask for action. "Oh, yes, we are selling our house . . . great house, you'll love it. It's a beautiful Colonial only one mile from the lake. We hate to part with it, but we are being transferred out-of-town. We love the neighborhood . . . how about stopping by Sunday afternoon around 2 P.M."

PREPLAN THE HOUSE TOUR

Don't let the prospect wander through your house alone. You should always guide him on the tour. Carefully think through the various ways in which you can show someone through your house. Prearrange the tour to emphasize the positive features of your house at the beginning and the end of the tour. Start and end positively. If there are negatives, sandwich them in-between.

If you have a comfortable porch or a large family room with a fireplace, plan to take the prospect there during your initial discussions. Tour the other rooms and end up in your modernized kitchen. Don't avoid the bad features. They will eventually be discovered and kill the sale if the prospect is surprised with them at a later date. Be prepared to open any closets. Also be ready for a full inspection of the attic and basement.

REMEMBER THE LAST-MINUTE TOUCHES

Turn off the TV. Nothing is more distracting than the last five minutes of a good mystery movie. Turn the telephone down to its softest ring.

Pets can annoy prospects. Some people may not be pet lovers. Others may find pet odors annoying or may even be allergic to your furry friends.

The aroma of baking bread or cookies is the only scent that should meet the prospect. You may not be a baker but you can buy frozen bread dough at the supermarket and turn on the oven. Create a home atmosphere with a pot of coffee, a bowl of fruit, a vase of fresh flowers. Home decorating magazines will give you plenty of themes.

If you're showing your house in the winter, build a fire in the fireplace. Buy an extra lamp to brighten dark corners.

Kids are not part of the selling process, so arrange a place for them to play when you have appointments.

APPEAL TO YOUR PROSPECT'S NEEDS

You have met your prospect at the door with a warm smile and a definite air of self-confidence. You have directed him to the most comfortable room in your house. Now you must engage in your first face-to-face conversation. It is at this point that you must determine the needs and desires of your prospect. The basic human needs were discussed earlier as security, affection, prestige, and self-expression. In preparing your newspaper ad, you have studied your house and developed an understanding of how your house can help fulfill each of these needs. Now you must determine which one of these needs is most important to your prospect and concentrate on those features of your house that appeal to this need.

The buyer's situation when he arrives will give you some indication of these needs. If he has his family with him, you will immediately get an indication of the influence that his family has on his need for security and affection. If he is driving an expensive car you will get an indication of his need for prestige.

ASK THE RIGHT QUESTIONS

Determine the ages of each of the prospects' children. This will give you an opportunity to draw attention to those features of your house and neighborhood that have special appeal to their children. Don't stress these features immediately, but as you conduct your tour, refer to those that may not be readily apparent to the prospect.

Ask where the prospect lives and why he is interested in moving. His answers may help you identify his need for prestige. If he is relocating to be closer to his job, it may help you evaluate his requirement for public transportation or driving distance to work. You can then concentrate on the locational benefits of your house.

Only ask a few questions. Be sincerely interested in him and in his family, but don't pry into his personal life. Observe his responses carefully.

Ask those questions that require a positive response. If you yourself are an avid gardener, you might ask the question, "Are you a gardener?" This appears to be a fairly straightforward question, however, it may result in embarrassment to the prospect if his answer must be "no." It would be better to ask, "Don't you think the garden is beautiful?" Then he can truthfully answer with a positive "yes."

If you are close to a golf course and ask the question "Do you play golf?" you might get an answer like, "No, ever since I've had this bad case of arthritis, I'm unable to play." Limit your questions to just a few that will almost always get a positive answer.

"A fire certainly feels good on a cold night, doesn't it?"

"Don't you think the paneled rathskeller has plenty of room for a Ping-Pong table?"

"Wouldn't that corner of the patio make a great spot for a barbecue pit?"

Properly phrased questions will help you in the following ways:

1. The prospect develops a feeling of being important. He feels that you are interested in his viewpoint and respect his opinion. He will then be more likely to respect *your* opinion.
2. Questions draw out the prospect's needs and desires. Properly phrased questions will eventually bring his own needs to the surface.
3. Asking questions helps you avoid talking too much. You should be the listener and by asking questions you will avoid overtalking and overselling.
4. Asking questions will help you avoid arguments. Rattling on about a subject will not only distract your listener but may create an argument.

DON'T OVERSELL

As the owner you may have a tendency to oversell. Restrain yourself. Listen to the buyer's comments and then put your emphasis on those features that will help satisfy his needs. Don't continually stress how the house satisfied your needs. *Your* needs are not *his* needs. Be concerned about *his* needs.

Don't oversell the outstanding features, most will speak for themselves. If there are hidden features (such as a large storage area in the attic, or a wine cellar in the basement), don't hesitate to show excitement . . . but don't oversell.

BE A GOOD LISTENER

Don't forget what has almost become a lost art. *Be a good listener*. Always let the other person know that you are sincerely interested in what he is saying. Give him every indication that you are trying to satisfy his needs. Listen!

BE BRIEF

If you are asked questions, give a brief, candid answer. Don't beat around the bush. Don't be negative. Be positive and enthusiastic. As a salesman you can never *know* too much, but you can *talk* too much.

Remember that the most important part of salesmanship is to find out what the other fellow wants, then help him find the best way to get it. Find out what your prospect wants, then convince him that your house can help him satisfy his desires.

KEEP YOUR COOL

You have discovered your prospect's needs through questioning. You have made every attempt during the house tour to appeal to these needs. Now you must bring your prospect to the right state of mind so that he is ready to buy.

It would be highly unlikely for your prospect to make one tour through your house, and immediately sign the contract. You will probably be visited three or four times by the prospect, with his family and friends, before you reach the final point of closing the sale. During this time, remember some of these key points:

1. Be gentle with your prospect. Don't use high-pressure techniques. If you attempt to rush him into a sale, you may antagonize him and lose the sale. Remember that purchasing a house is probably one of the most important financial steps in his life. It is only normal for a buyer to take his time and exercise caution.

2. As you reach the final stage of negotiation, don't let the prospect get you into an argument. Keep your composure. Don't let your desire to win an argument on a small point lose the sale. Your purpose is not to demonstrate your effectiveness in negotiating or your ability to debate, but to sell your house. Don't win the battle and lose the war!

3. Continue to show confidence throughout the entire period that you are dealing with your prospect. Don't express doubt or uncertainty. Be proud of your house and proud of yourself. Keep your temper and never lose your patience.

4. If the prospect makes an unfavorable comment about your house, accept it. Don't defend your house; especially if the comment is in an area of personal

taste. Acknowledge that certain things in the house could be improved, or that different people have a different way of living.

5. Don't appear to act superior and leave him with the impression that you are condescending to his level. If you express confidence, it will be transmitted to your prospect and he will have confidence in you, in himself, and in the purchase of your house. Don't do anything to destroy his confidence in himself.

6. Empathize with your buyer. Throughout your dealing with the prospect always mentally sit on his side of the table. Find out why he is taking certain action. By putting yourself in his place, and understanding his feelings, you may have an opportunity to overcome his objections.

OVERCOME OBJECTIONS

Salesmen know that they will close only one out of every ten sales without having to overcome some objections along the way. Consider the amount of money the prospect is going to invest in your house and you will understand why he will have certain doubts and fears. He expresses these doubts and fears in the form of objections. Many of these objections will not be real, but rather, symptoms of the caution that he feels he must exercise in making this important decision.

A good salesman has no fear of objections. He is not only prepared for them, he welcomes them. The prospect who wanders through your house admiring your furniture, artifacts, and Oriental rugs is probably just a "looker." He has no real interest in buying. The buyer who raises objections about the number of closets or the lack of a garbage disposal is probably expressing these objections because he is seriously thinking about purchasing your house.

Be prepared for these objections by comparing your house with other houses. Look for disadvantages or shortcomings and be prepared to overcome objections when they are raised. When the buyer raises objections you have an immediate clue to his needs through some of the dissatisfactions that he is expressing. There are several ways to handle objections.

1. *Overcome the objection with an affirmative answer.* If you are showing the prospect through the house and he notices that some of the closets are small, but has not yet seen the ample storage space in the attic, make a very positive statement by saying, "Yes, the closet space in some rooms does appear small, but it is more than ample when you consider the large storage area we have in the attic. We find it more practical to have our clothes cleaned, pressed, and stored in the attic for the winter. We then only have one season of clothes in our closets, and we find there is more than ample space."

2. *Change the subject.* If the prospect mentions a deficiency and there is clearly no way to overcome it, don't dwell on the subject. Nod your head in acknowledgment and change the subject.

3. *Make the objection appear minor in relation to the other qualities of the house.* The prospect may object to the lack of a fireplace. This may be a valid objection in his mind. Try to overcome it by acknowledging it as an objection, but make it appear to be a minor point in relationship to the other qualities. Your answer might be, "Yes, in some houses a fireplace is a definite asset, but we have always found this house warm and cozy and take special delight in our large

family room. We have had many delightful parties for our young teenage son that have helped make this a great house to live in."

If the prospect raises objections, be forthright and honest and don't evade the question. Admit that the house has certain faults and stress ways that these faults can be overcome. Never lie or create any reason for the prospect to mistrust you.

Whatever method you use to answer the prospect's objections make certain you always listen very carefully. These objections may point out the needs of your prospect. You can then concentrate on his needs and move toward closing the sale. These objections may be the key to your sale.

CLOSE THE SALE

Once the prospect begins to make semiaffirmative statements such as "Maybe I should consider it," "It looks pretty good," "I think I'll talk it over with my wife," you have reached the point where you should stop selling. Your prospect has probably made a decision to go ahead. Any good salesman understands that once he gets this signal the prospect is making a mental commitment and he should stop selling and stress closing.

It does you no good to go over and over the good points of the house if the prospect has already acknowledged that he is interested. Your next step is to settle on the price and work out the details of closing.

Chapters 6 and 7 will discuss the financing and legal consideration of closing. But before you study the mechanics of closing there is one last step necessary. The prospect has made a decision to purchase your house but you have not settled on the exact price. Before you enter into negotiations on price, remember that *in a successful negotiation everybody wins*. Both buyer and seller should go to the closing thinking they got the best deal possible.

Your negotiations on price should not take the form of haggling. You are not dealing with a used-car salesman. The price you have quoted should not be discussed as your *asking price* but as your *firm price*. If your house is listed for $150,000, that is your price. If asked whether you will come down, don't say "yes." If your answer is "yes" or "we might consider $140,000" you will probably get a bid not for $150,000, but for $140,000. Your response of $140,000 has now become the asking price. Your $150,000 original asking price is gone forever.

The best statement to make in handling the negotiation for price is to request that the prospect submit a contract. If the contract is not satisfactory, tell him you will either turn it down within twenty-four hours or make a counter proposal. Tell him that you are not prepared at this time to make a decision or mention another price. You will consider his offer and give him an answer within twenty-four hours. You can say that your price is $150,000 and you really haven't given much thought to a lower price. Blame your request for a written contract on your lawyer. Say that you were advised to get a firm offer in writing, with earnest money, and will talk it over with your lawyer after you have received the contract.

CHECK LIST
SELLING TECHNIQUES

☐ BE ENTHUSIASTIC

☐ SHOW SELF-CONFIDENCE

☐ LOOK SUCCESSFUL

☐ BE POSITIVE

☐ BE CHEERFUL

☐ KNOW YOUR HOUSE

☐ KNOW YOUR NEIGHBORHOOD

☐ ASK QUESTIONS

☐ DON'T OVERSELL

☐ BE A GOOD LISTENER

☐ BE BRIEF

☐ BE CANDID

☐ DON'T TALK TOO MUCH

☐ DON'T HIGH PRESSURE

☐ AVOID ARGUMENTS

☐ DON'T LOSE YOUR PATIENCE

☐ DON'T EXPRESS DOUBT

☐ EMPATHIZE WITH YOUR BUYER

CHECK LIST
HOW TO SHOW YOUR HOUSE

☐ FOLLOW RULES OF GOOD SALESMANSHIP

☐ KNOW YOUR TERRITORY

☐ SELL WHEN THE TELEPHONE RINGS

☐ PREPLAN THE HOUSE TOUR

☐ REMEMBER THE LAST-MINUTE TOUCHES

☐ APPEAL TO YOUR PROSPECT'S NEEDS

☐ ASK THE RIGHT QUESTIONS

☐ DON'T OVERSELL

☐ BE A GOOD LISTENER

☐ BE BRIEF

☐ KEEP YOUR COOL

☐ OVERCOME OBJECTIONS

☐ CLOSE THE SALE

CHAPTER 6

FOR SALE

HOW A KNOWLEDGE OF FINANCING WILL HELP YOUR SALE

BY OWNER

M ost houses are financed since few buyers have the full cash price available to them in savings and, in addition, a home loan represents about the cheapest kind of credit available to individuals. If a buyer has a 25 percent or more downpayment for a conventional home loan, the interest rate is almost competitive with the rates currently paid by many large corporate borrowers. Conventional loan rates have averaged from 8½ percent to 11½ percent in recent years. Compare this with the 18 percent paid on credit-card borrowing, or 12 percent paid on a car loan.

The home loan is not only a desirable method of borrowing, but has become an indispensable element in the transfer of a home. A knowledge of home financing can, therefore, be an important element in selling your house.

To help your sale you should anticipate your buyer's finance questions. "How large a downpayment do I need?" "What interest rate and terms are available?" "What will my monthly payments be?" "How much do I need to earn to get a loan of this size?" This chapter will show you how to answer these questions quickly and with the confidence that your answers are correct and up-to-date.

As you discuss home financing you may hear many new terms: mortgage loan, first deed, trust deed, deed of trust, or first lien. They all mean basically the same thing . . . "home loan." It is best not to discuss these technical terms, but to simply use the words "home loan." Everybody knows what a home loan is. The others are technical terms of local usage. While they make you sound knowledgeable, they may confuse your buyer. If you say "I've talked to the people at Highwater Savings and they will make a 10 percent, twenty-five year *home loan* to the right buyer" . . . you will get your message across. Try to keep it simple and communicate as effectively as possible.

THE HOME LOAN MARKET

When there is an adequate supply of home-loan funds there is competition among lenders. Loans are larger, longer, and cheaper. Many lending institutions are authorized to lend up to 80 percent of the appraised value or sale price (whichever is lower) and, when ample funds are available, they will frequently advance the maximum amount their lending rules allow. A strong home-loan market will obviously help your sale.

Assume you are selling in a strong home-loan market. You sign a contract for $100,000 and the buyer goes to a lender for his loan. The maximum conventional loan he could obtain would probably be around $80,000 or 80 percent of the selling price. He would need $20,000, or 20 percent in cash to pay the balance of the purchase price above the loan amount. Assume the interest rate is 10 percent payable over twenty-five years. The buyer's monthly payment for principal and interest would be $727 (see Appendix 1), plus a deposit for taxes and insurance. If the lender requires that the buyer only spend 25 percent of his gross annual income on financing his house, the buyer would have to earn $44,496 to qualify for the loan under these strong home-loan market conditions. Refer to line 2 on the chart on page 147 for this calculation.

Weak home-loan market conditions would change the situation. In the above example, tightening of loan terms from twenty-five years to twenty years, increasing the interest rate from 10 percent to 10½ percent, and reducing the total amount of the loan available from 80 percent to 75 percent would disqualify the buyer earning $44,496. The changing market conditions causing these moderately unfavorable adjustments, could force you to find a buyer who earns at least $45,552 or more a year, instead of one who earns $44,496. In addition, your buyer would now need $25,000 in cash for a downpayment instead of $20,000. Refer to line 6 on the chart on page 147 for this calculation.

There are simply fewer people in the economy who earn the additional salary required, and also have the additional $5,000 in cash for a downpayment. Something would obviously have to give. Since there are fewer buyers competing for your house, it will probably take you longer to sell or you may be forced to sell at a lower price.

The lenders you will contact will help you understand your present home loan market. *Remember that in a strong home-loan market you can afford to bargain harder and hold out longer. In a weak market you should be prepared to give a little more.* (Defending yourself in a weak market will be discussed later in this chapter.)

CONVENTIONAL LOANS

Banks, savings and loan associations, and mutual savings banks are the principal sources of conventional loans. The lender makes a conventional loan without support of insurance against loss of principal. Since the loan is not insured, and the lender can look only to the property and homeowner to reduce his risk, he will require the buyer to make a downpayment of 20 percent to 25 percent. The large downpayment reduces the risk to the lender in cases where the buyer may default on the loan at a later date. Conventional loans run at the current home-loan interest rates for a term of up to forty years.

INSURED CONVENTIONAL LOANS

A privately insured conventional loan is just like a conventional loan, except the lender requires less downpayment because a private insurer guarantees repayment of the riskiest part of the loan . . . the top 20 percent. This insurance is usually purchased by buyers who have only a small downpayment, for example 10 percent. Both the property and the buyer must qualify and it usually takes a few days to have the lender appraise the house and check the buyer's credit. The cost of this insurance varies but a typical program might include a charge of ½ of 1 percent of the loan amount payable at closing, and ¼ of 1 percent payable for the next eight years. Interest rates on the home loan are at the current market.

ARM—ADJUSTABLE RATE MORTGAGE

Your buyer may be interested in an ARM, adjustable rate mortgage, which is also known as the AML (adjustable mortgage loan), the AIM (adjustable interest mortgage), or VRM (variable rate mortgage).

Adjustable rate mortgages (ARMs) have initially lower

interest rates, but vary over the long term. Interest rates and monthly payments are changed at intervals. The initial interest rate and subsequent adjustments to it reflect periodic changes in a specified "index." An example of such are yields on U.S. Treasury securities or the prevailing prime lending rate.

The period over which your buyer will pay back the loan is divided into rate adjustment periods, at which time the interest rate is recomputed. In some cases, limitations or "caps" prevent the rate change from exceeding a specified increase or decrease from the base rate, despite the severity of index changes. This cap feature limits the potential positive or negative impact on the monthly mortgage payment which might result from fluctuating interest rates.

ARMs are complicated mortgages and it is advisable to read the "small print" and thoroughly understand all aspects of the mortgage. Your buyer will require a full "briefing" from the savings and loan offering the ARM.

FHA LOANS

You may have to consider an FHA insured loan if your house is old or located in the "inner city" of a large metropolitan area. When you talk to lenders you will find out at once whether they consider your house an FHA candidate. If they do, this may be the only home loan your buyer will be able to get.

If it is necessary to sell your house with FHA financing you should take several steps before you put your house on the market. Contact either a bank, savings and loan association or a mortgage banker who writes FHA insured loans in your area. He will advise you to obtain an FHA appraisal, which can take anywhere from two to six weeks. The FHA appraised value will be the maximum amount you can get for your house, unless your buyer signs a separate declaration advising that he agrees to pay more than the FHA appraised value.

FHA insured loans sometimes have an interest rate fixed below the current market interest rate and the lender, therefore, requires an additional fee called "points." One point equals 1 percent of the loan amount. The FHA requires that the seller, *not* the buyer, pay the points. In prior years the seller could simply raise the asking price by the value of the points and, in effect, the buyer was paying the points. Under the present FHA regulations, the house must be appraised at the market value and the seller is stuck with the points.

FHA insured loans are a bureaucrat's delight of forms, tricky regulations, confusion, and unforeseen complications. Remember these rules:

1. If you are asked to sign a contract, be certain the buyer applies for credit qualification at once. If he is not approved in two weeks, you should have the option to back out of the sales contract.
2. Know what house repairs you must make to satisfy the FHA and be prepared to make them.
3. Calculate the cost of points and other loan expenses you have to pay. Make certain that these are satisfactory to you before you sign the contract. You should discuss these costs with your lawyer and know all of the requirements that have to be met to satisfy the FHA.

COMPLETE THE "MORTGAGE SHOPPER'S GUIDE"

The recent trend is toward a greater number of conventional and insured conventional loans and fewer FHA loans. A conventional loan, even if privately insured, involves less red tape, can be made in a couple of weeks, and is usually less expensive to the buyer and the seller.

Most houses qualify for a conventional home loan. Call home lenders and ask if they are making conventional loans in your neighborhood. You'll find out quickly, because, if they aren't interested they will tell you. Since different lenders have different lending practices and policies, call several. If they are making conventional loans in your neighborhood, then continue asking for further information about the conventional loan terms offered. If they are not, an FHA insured loan will probably be needed. (The remainder of this chapter assumes your buyer will finance with a conventional rather than an FHA loan.)

Banks, savings and loan associations, and mutual savings banks are the best places to start looking for a conventional loan. They are members of your community and want their home-loan customers to become savings-account customers and also take advantage of their other services.

Call your bank first to discuss the current terms available in the home-loan market. Ask your banker if he is interested in making a home loan on a house in your neighborhood. Describe the size, age, and price range of your house. Your banker is in the business of making these loans and he should be glad to talk to you about their current terms. If he won't make a loan because of bank policy or because the bank doesn't make loans in your area, he can tell you whom you should call. Your lawyer may also be able to recommend a home-loan officer at one or more of the local lending institutions.

You should call three or four banks and savings institutions both downtown and in the suburbs. They will tell you, in general, the maximum amount of the loan they would make for a house in your price range, the interest rate, and the term (or number of years) over which the loan would be repaid. They will also tell you the monthly principal and interest payments required (or you can refer to Appendix 1).

Five Mortgage Shopper's Guides are provided at the end of this chapter to help you gather this loan data. Before you call the lending institutions, enter the price you expect to receive for your house under "Selling Price" on the Mortgage Shopper's Guide. Then calculate the down-payment amount for payment ranges from 50 percent to 15 percent and enter under "Downpayment." Subtract the down payment from the selling price and enter the difference under "Loan Amount." This is the amount the buyer must borrow based on the various down-payment amounts.

Ask the loan officer for the interest rates and terms (length of loan in years) under these various down-payment amounts. Enter this data under "Interest Rate" and "Term" on the Mortgage Shopper's Guide.

On conventional loans you may get a quote of an interest rate plus "points." The points are an additional fee charged by the lender to process the loan. One "point" equals 1 percent of the loan amount. For example, if the loan amount is $40,000, one point equals $400 and two points equal $800. One point is the customary charge to the buyer in many areas. Enter the point charge under "Points" on the Mortgage Shopper's Guide.

Using the table in Appendix 1 you can find the monthly interest and principal payment necessary to amortize the various loan amounts, interest rates, and terms you have entered on the Guide. Enter this payment amount under "Monthly P & I."

Entering insured conventional loan data involves the same steps as for regular conventional loans, with the exception of an additional charge for the insurance premium. This expense will be quoted to you as a percentage rate similar to the interest rate. Add the interest rate and the insurance premium rate and enter the total under "Interest Rate."

The loan data you have gathered on your Mortgage Shopper's Guide will prove to be a valuable asset to both you and your buyer.

DISCUSS FINANCING WITH YOUR BUYER

You have now landed a buyer who wants to sign a contract. However, before you sign, both you and the buyer should discuss his financial qualifications. Your buyer will naturally be concerned with making the down payment, and also will want to know how much his monthly principal and interest payments will be. You, on the other hand, will be interested in the buyer's loan eligibility. It would be unwise to take your house off the market for two or three weeks, while your buyer shops for a loan, without first discussing these financial considerations.

It may be difficult to get your buyer to discuss his personal finances, but if you point out the advantage to him (anticipating his down payment and his monthly payments) he will probably open up. Review the Mortgage Shopper's Guides with your buyer and then ask him to fill out a Loan Qualification Chart. (Completing the chart is discussed later in this chapter.) You can work together or separately. If he prefers to fill out a Loan Qualification Chart by himself he can simply tell you that he "does or does not qualify" and will not have to reveal his personal finances to you.

In certain situations you may determine your buyer is only marginally qualified for a loan on your house. In this case, don't reject his contract, but ask him to see a home-loan officer for a preliminary discussion of his qualifications before you sign.

You may not have the opportunity to work with your buyer on the financial aspects of the sale, but may simply receive a sales contract, which allows the buyer a certain period of time to find a loan (see Chapter 7). If you have no information on which to judge the financial qualifications of the buyer, make certain you restrict the period of time he has to find a loan to the shortest, yet reasonable, period. In completing the Mortgage Shopper's Guides you will have gathered information on the normal processing time a lender requires, so use this data as a guideline. Don't take your house off the market for three weeks if your buyer can get a loan commitment from a lender in five days. The loss of this valuable marketing time may be very costly.

THE QUALIFICATION PROCESS

You will have a better understanding of the qualification process if you know the tests a lender considers. Since the lender is being asked to extend credit for twenty to thirty years, he will naturally be very concerned with his security, which is made up of equal parts of the *long-term value of the house* and the *buyer's ability to repay the loan*.

As a measurement of the *long-term value of the house,* lenders use a loan test called "loan to value ratio" . . . the percentage of the home loan to the lender's appraised value of the property. A house appraised at $100,000 with an 80 percent "loan to value ratio" would qualify for a loan of $80,000. The down payment would then be the balance of the purchase price, 20 percent, or $20,000. By applying this ratio, lenders assure repayment of the loan without much risk if the buyer is later forced to sell the house because he can't carry the payments.

Before making a loan the lender will have your house appraised. If you have had a professional appraisal, you can probably assume that the lender's appraised value will be close to your appraised value. If your selling price is close to the appraised value, you can assume the lender will accept your selling price as a reasonable measure of value.

The *buyer's ability to repay the loan* will be determined by the amount, source, and stability of his income, and part or all of his wife's income, together with their credit history and cash reserves. Each lender has his own rules for acceptability of income and credit. Basically, however, a home borrower with good credit can usually pay 20 percent of his gross income for home-loan principal, interest, taxes, and insurance. If the borrower has no long term installment obligations (longer than nine months), the lender may consider up to 25 percent of the borrower's income as available for loan payments.

More liberal extensions might be available to a young professional with satisfactory employment history, if he can reasonably point to quick gains in future earnings. Home lenders can recognize the expectancy of these improved earnings by making a larger loan. Another example of preferred treatment might be a mature, steady employee in his middle years whose family obligations are nearly complete. He will need less of his income to satisfy family obligations so a lender may consider more of his income as available for loan payments.

Assume your selling price is $100,000 and your buyer is paying $20,000 or 20 percent down. He then needs an $80,000 or 80 percent loan. If your monthly real estate tax and insurance expense is $200, it must be added to the amount of monthly principal and interest to determine the buyer's total monthly loan payment. Assume also that you review your Mortgage Shopper's Guides and determine that a buyer could get a 10 percent interest, twenty-five-year loan if he could put $20,000 or 20 percent down.

The chart on the following page shows the relationship of the down payment to the buyer's required gross annual salary. On line 2 you can see that, for the above assumptions, the monthly principal and interest expense is $727. If you add $200 for taxes and insurance the total monthly payment is $927. Multiply by 12 to arrive at an annual payment amount of $11,124. Multiply again by 4 (asssuming he can borrow up to 25 percent of his gross annual salary) to arrive at $44,496, which is the amount of gross annual salary the buyer must earn to be eligible for a 10 percent interest, twenty-five-year conventional loan.

The chart also indicates the various relationships that can exist between the buyer's down payment and his required gross annual salary. If the buyer has a smaller down payment, his loan amount and monthly payment amount will increase. He will also be required to earn a higher gross annual salary to support the larger payments. As the chart indicates, if the down payment is under 20 percent, the lender may require the buyer to earn five times the annual payment rather than four times.

COMPLETE A LOAN QUALIFICATION CHART

Five Loan Qualification Charts are provided at the end of this chapter to use when you work with your buyer. The example mentioned above is recorded on a Loan Qualification Chart below.

Completing a Loan Qualification Chart may save valuable

RELATIONSHIP OF DOWN PAYMENT TO BUYER'S REQUIRED GROSS ANNUAL SALARY

10% — 25 years

Selling Price	Down Payment	%	Loan Amount	Monthly P & I	Tax and Insurance	Monthly Payment	Annual Payment	Required Gross Annual Salary
$100,000	$25,000	25	$75,000	682	200	$ 882 x 12	10,584 x 4	$42,336
100,000	20,000	20	80,000	727	200	927 x 12	11,124 x 4	44,496
100,000	15,000	15	85,000	772	200	972 x 12	11,664 x 4	46,656
100,000	10,000	10	90,000	818	200	1,018 x 12	12,216 x 4	48,864

10½%—20 Years

Selling Price	Down Payment	%	Loan Amount	Monthly P & I	Tax and Insurance	Monthly Payment	Annual Payment	Required Gross Annual Salary
$100,000	$25,000	25	$75,000	749	200	$ 949 x 12	11,388 x 4	$45,552
100,000	20,000	20	80,000	799	200	999 x 12	11,988 x 4	47,952
100,000	15,000	15	85,000	849	200	1,049 x 12	12,588 x 4	50,352
100,000	10,000	10	90,000	898	200	1,098 x 12	13,176 x 4	52,704

time for both you and the buyer, if he can determine that he does not have either the required down payment or the income to support the monthly payments.

Loan Qualification Chart

Purchase price	$100,000
Less: down payment 20%	20,000
Equals: loan amount	80,000
Monthly principal and interest	727
Plus: monthly taxes and insurance	200
Equals: total monthly payment	927
Times: 12 months	× 12
Equals: annual payment	11,124
Times: 4	× 4
Equals: required gross annual salary	$44,496

DEFEND YOURSELF IN A WEAK LOAN MARKET

When an adequate supply of home loan funds is not available, you may have a difficult time getting your price. You may have to use one of the following techniques if you want to sell your house quickly and at a figure near your target price.

1. *Pledged savings account.* If your buyer needs an additional 5 percent down payment at a $100,000 selling price, he needs $5,000. Banks and savings and loan associations are authorized to make loans against passbook savings accounts. If you agree to deposit $5,000 (the difference between what the buyer has

available and what he needs), the lender may consider making the loan against the security of both the house and your savings account.

When the buyer pays the loan down to an acceptable limit, where the lender would have the loan anyway, you will get your savings back. This can take several years. Meanwhile, if the buyer does not make his payments on the loan, the lender is authorized to use the amount in the savings account to protect itself against loss. You will have to rely on the buyer to be repaid the amounts withdrawn by the lender. Many times the buyer will give you a second mortgage in this situation.

2. *Second mortgage.* Second mortgages are usually considered only where a buyer has a very strong income and the purchase price is generous enough to warrant keeping your funds in the transaction.

3. *Sell on contract.* You might consider the idea of selling your house on contract to the buyer, taking his payments, and paying your own mortgage. The buyer would be given the deed on your property only when he had made the last payment on the contract. These contracts are usually made for five to seven years and the buyer is required to refinance the contract when he has paid enough principal to become eligible for a regular home loan. Your security is your house plus the buyer's down payment.

There can be both economic and legal problems associated with selling your house on contract or with taking a second mortgage. You should discuss these with your lawyer before you decide to undertake these risks.

4. *Loan assumption.* If the loan on your house represents 75 percent or more of your target price, and has

twenty or more years to run, you might want to consider allowing your loan to be assumed. The buyer assuming your loan often gets a lower interest rate and saves the loan closing costs.

Before allowing your loan to be assumed, you should understand that you will probably remain personally responsible for the obligation. If the buyer defaults on the payment of the loan it will be your default too. Your lender can probably proceed against you for the difference he does not get from your buyer. Discuss this with your lawyer if you are considering this approach.

CHECK LIST

HOW A KNOWLEDGE OF FINANCING WILL HELP YOUR SALE

☐ THE HOME LOAN MARKET

☐ CONVENTIONAL LOANS

☐ INSURED CONVENTIONAL LOANS

☐ FHA LOAN

☐ COMPLETE THE ''MORTGAGE SHOPPER'S GUIDE ''

☐ DISCUSS FINANCING WITH YOUR BUYER

☐ THE QUALIFICATION PROCESS

☐ COMPLETE A LOAN QUALIFICATION CHART

☐ DEFEND YOURSELF IN A WEAK LOAN MARKET

LOAN QUALIFICATION CHART

Purchase price $_____

Less: down payment ____%   _____

Equals: loan amount   _____

Monthly principal and interest   _____

Plus: monthly taxes and insurance   _____

Equals: total monthly payment   _____

Times: 12 months   ___x12___

Equals: annual payment   _____

Times: 4   ___x4___

Equals: required gross annual salary   _____

LOAN QUALIFICATION CHART

Purchase price $_____

Less: down payment ____%   _____

Equals: loan amount   _____

Monthly principal and interest   _____

Plus: monthly taxes and insurance   _____

Equals: total monthly payment   _____

Times: 12 months   ___x12___

Equals: annual payment   _____

Times: 4   ___x4___

Equals: required gross annual salary $_____

MORTGAGE SHOPPER'S GUIDE

Name of lending institution _____   **Telephone number** _____

Address / Branch _____   **Talked to** _____

Processing time from application to commitment: _____ **days. Commitment to closing:** _____ **days. Times borrower must earn conventional loan payment:** _____ **times. Insured:** _____ **times.**

Conventional Loan

Selling Price	Down-Payment	%	Loan Amount	Interest Rate	Term	Monthly P & I	Points
____	____	50	____	____	____	____	____
____	____	25	____	____	____	____	____
____	____	20	____	____	____	____	____
____	____	15	____	____	____	____	____
____	____	__					

Insured Conventional Loan

Selling Price	Down-Payment	%	Loan Amount	Interest Rate	Term	Monthly P & I	Points
____	____	15	____	____	____	____	____
____	____	10	____	____	____	____	____
____	____	5	____	____	____	____	____
____	____	__					

MORTGAGE SHOPPER'S GUIDE

Name of lending institution _____ Telephone number _____
Address / Branch _____ Talked to _____

Processing time from application to commitment: _____ days. Commitment to closing: _____ days. Times borrower must earn conventional loan payment: _____ times. Insured: _____ times.

Conventional Loan

Selling Price	Down-Payment	%	Loan Amount	Interest Rate	Term	Monthly P & I	Points
_____	_____	50	_____	_____	_____	_____	_____
_____	_____	25	_____	_____	_____	_____	_____
_____	_____	20	_____	_____	_____	_____	_____
_____	_____	15	_____	_____	_____	_____	_____
_____	_____	__	_____	_____	_____	_____	_____

Insured Conventional Loan

Selling Price	Down-Payment	%	Loan Amount	Interest Rate	Term	Monthly P & I	Points
_____	_____	15	_____	_____	_____	_____	_____
_____	_____	10	_____	_____	_____	_____	_____
_____	_____	5	_____	_____	_____	_____	_____
_____	_____	__	_____	_____	_____	_____	_____

MORTGAGE SHOPPER'S GUIDE

Name of lending institution _____

Telephone number _____

Address / Branch _____

Talked to _____

Processing time from application to commitment: _____ days. Commitment to closing: _____ days. Times borrower must earn conventional loan payment: _____ times. Insured: _____ times.

Conventional Loan

Selling Price	Down-Payment	%	Loan Amount	Interest Rate	Term	Monthly P & I	Points
____	____	50	____	____	____	____	____
____	____	25	____	____	____	____	____
____	____	20	____	____	____	____	____
____	____	15	____	____	____	____	____
____	____	____					

Insured Conventional Loan

____	____	15	____	____	____	____	____
____	____	10	____	____	____	____	____
____	____	5	____	____	____	____	____
____	____	____					

MORTGAGE SHOPPER'S GUIDE

Name of lending institution _____ Telephone number _____
Address / Branch _____ Talked to _____

Processing time from application to commitment: _____ days. Commitment to closing: _____ days. Times
borrower must earn conventional loan payment: _____ times. Insured: _____ times.

Conventional Loan

Selling Price	Down-Payment	%	Loan Amount	Interest Rate	Term	Monthly P & I	Points
_____	_____	50	_____	_____	_____	_____	_____
_____	_____	25	_____	_____	_____	_____	_____
_____	_____	20	_____	_____	_____	_____	_____
_____	_____	15	_____	_____	_____	_____	_____
_____	_____	—	_____				

Insured Conventional Loan

Selling Price	Down-Payment	%	Loan Amount	Interest Rate	Term	Monthly P & I	Points
_____	_____	15	_____	_____	_____	_____	_____
_____	_____	10	_____	_____	_____	_____	_____
_____	_____	5	_____	_____	_____	_____	_____
_____	_____	—	_____				

MORTGAGE SHOPPER'S GUIDE

Name of lending institution _____

Address / Branch _____

Telephone number _____

Talked to _____

Processing time from application to commitment: _____ days. Commitment to closing: _____ days. Times borrower must earn conventional loan payment: _____ times. Insured: _____ times.

Conventional Loan

Selling Price	Down-Payment	%	Loan Amount	Interest Rate	Term	Monthly P & I	Points
_____	_____	50	_____	_____	_____	_____	_____
_____	_____	25	_____	_____	_____	_____	_____
_____	_____	20	_____	_____	_____	_____	_____
_____	_____	15	_____	_____	_____	_____	_____
_____	_____	—					

Insured Conventional Loan

Selling Price	Down-Payment	%	Loan Amount	Interest Rate	Term	Monthly P & I	Points
_____	_____	15	_____	_____	_____	_____	_____
_____	_____	10	_____	_____	_____	_____	_____
_____	_____	5	_____	_____	_____	_____	_____
_____	_____	—					

CHAPTER
7

FOR

HOW YOUR LAWYER
WILL HELP
YOUR SALE

SALE

BY OWNER

As the seller, your whole effort is aimed at finding a buyer interested in your house, and then drawing up a binding contract that will state the terms of your sales agreement clearly and accurately. You can agree with your buyer on the price and other terms, but then come the problems! Deeds, title evidence, tenders, defaults, cures, third-party performance, risk of loss, implied agreements, mandatory agreements, and other issues too numerous to mention.

Your lawyer will know about these and the many other legal issues that pertain to your contract. His job is to direct attention to the legal aspects of your sale, protect your bargain, record it properly and then efficiently bring together the miscellaneous details in a sales contract.

His job also is to inform you of alternatives, safeguards, and simplifications that can aid you in reaching an agreement with your buyer. He will help you reach a safe, practical, and binding agreement.

The following material is not intended to replace your lawyer's advice. Neither is it intended to treat this subject other than in a general and practical light. It is offered primarily to prepare you to discuss pertinent problems with your lawyer and to help you understand some of the decisions that you must make with his consultation. It should *not* be used as a substitute for your lawyer's experienced advice.

HIRE A LAWYER EXPERIENCED IN HOME SALES

After you find your buyer, your lawyer will be nine-tenths of your deal. He will draw your sales contract and hold the earnest money deposit in his trust account. He will guide your sale through the technical closing process. Even if you have sold your own house before, it is important to have expert help. Knowing a little law will not make you a lawyer any more than knowing a little first aid will make you a doctor. Both doctors and lawyers invest many years in study and experience to become efficient practitioners of their art.

Why is there so much mystery associated with real estate law? First of all, there is no uniform real estate law from state to state. Each state is free to make its own law with respect to the real estate within its own borders. Also, there are many different state and federal agencies that have authority to add to the collection of laws called "real estate law." Cities, counties, state legislatures, and state courts also create and add to the body of real estate laws.

In addition, there is another very important concept called "local custom." Each community in the country has a set of unwritten rules with respect to real estate that constitute "local custom." These rules and practices can and do vary from place to place. They relate to such ideas as: which terms of a contract are considered negotiable, the form and content of deeds and other documents, the meaning of certain words, what is considered "fair dealing," and many other matters.

Over the years, the generations of people who have shaped these rules have come and gone, but the customs and practices have continued to be used. The unwritten rules, agreements, and standards have now become, in effect, part of your local law. To protect yourself in closing the sale of your house, you should hire a lawyer experienced in your "local custom."

Your sale will progress from negotiation, to initial agreement on the basic terms of sale, to signing a written sales contract, probably to an escrow agreement, and, finally, to the closing documents.

Your title will be examined by both the buyer's and the lender's lawyers. If any title defects are found, they must be remedied by your lawyer. There are almost always a few defects or deviations that have to be corrected by affidavits or written statements. There may be legal problems when your title is examined if: you bought your house on contract, own it in a trust, acquired it through an estate, were recently divorced, had a judgment taken against you, or if you are in the middle of a hassle with the IRS. Your lawyer should be able to provide a solution to these problems, or offer a suitable alternative, so that your sale can be consummated.

To avoid time-consuming difficulties that may delay your sale, see your lawyer *before* you put your house on the market. If you retain his services early in your sale, your lawyer will know your needs before he is called on to act. Bring your listing sheet and title papers to your first meeting. He can then prepare himself to advise you properly.

Looking for a good lawyer experienced in home sales is not as difficult as it may seem. There are plenty of them around. Your job is to find one who is willing to work hard for you. "Working hard" may involve an evening or Saturday morning meeting with your buyer and his lawyer.

If you were represented by a lawyer when you bought your house, and were satisfied with his services, give him a call first. He probably made copies of your deed, title policy, survey, and other closing instruments. If you did not have a lawyer represent you when you bought your house, you should begin looking right away. Relatives, business associates, or neighbors who have received satisfactory service from an experienced lawyer are often good references.

You can also call your local bank or savings and loan association for referrals. Ask the amount of the legal fees usually charged a seller for a house in your price range. This may be a useful guide when you discuss fees with your lawyer.

At your first meeting, tell your lawyer that you are selling your house without a broker and expect him to draw up the contract, deed, and other necessary documents and also handle the title closing. Ask him what his fee will be to represent you throughout the transaction. Normally the guideline for his fee would be an amount equal to ½ to 1 percent of the sale price.

If you expect to sell with FHA financing, take back a second mortgage, were recently divorced, or have any other potential complications, tell your lawyer at the first meeting. If any of these conditions exist he may raise his fee because of the extra time involved in preparing the documents to remedy these special situations. Avoid misunderstandings. Be thorough and frank in your discussions with him. This way neither of you will be surprised about the work involved or fees to be charged.

THE SALES CONTRACT

There are several areas of agreement ordinarily covered in the sales contract.

1. The signatures of the buyer and seller
2. A description of the property to be sold:
   a. the real estate being sold, the lot, the house and the fixtures attached to the house
   b. personal property

3. The general agreement to buy on the part of the buyer and the general agreement to sell on the part of the seller
4. The purchase price and the financial terms of the sale: the amount of earnest money, the amount to be financed by the buyer, and the cash balance to be paid at the closing
5. A description of title evidence, deed, other transfer documents, and closing procedures
6. General agreements (based on "local custom," if applicable)
7. Special agreements that may apply to your sale: FHA provisions, rent to be paid for early possession, buyer's and seller's representation that neither employed a broker, representations regarding building violations, commonly used driveway, road easements, required repairs, etc.

Each of these areas of the contract are discussed in more detail below so you will have a basic foundation for understanding and intelligently discussing your contract with your lawyer and your buyer. (A blank sample contract form used in Illinois is shown at the end of this chapter.)

MAKE CERTAIN ALL PARTIES SIGN THE CONTRACT

If you are married, you probably own the title to your house jointly, so both you and your spouse should sign your contract. In many states, even if a spouse does not have an ownership interest in the property, marital laws may give the spouse rights with regard to the house. Your spouse should sign the agreement to show willingness to give up these rights.

If you bought your house on contract, inherited it, or own it in a trust, you may not presently have the authority to sign a deed. To avoid possible legal problems, the lawyer who handled these matters should be consulted.

Married buyers usually want to own their homes jointly, so both should sign the contract. Even if they are not taking the title jointly, both should sign since you may want to proceed against both of them if they try to back out. There are other reasons involving the credit worthiness of the buyers and their obligations to close the contract that make it important for both to sign.

Whether or not you should enter a contract with a straw party or nominee is a judgment you should make only after consultation with your lawyer.

PROPERLY DESCRIBE YOUR PROPERTY

The description of your property is one of the most important provisions of your contract. Take particular care to be sure your lawyer has everything he needs to describe your property accurately. Common sense dictates that the best description available should be used in your contract. This will avoid time-consuming errors and omissions that, in extreme cases, could completely defeat your sale.

The best description of your house is known as the ''legal description.'' This is the lot and block or survey description used in the abstract, title policy, plat of survey, or the deed you received when you bought your house. Your lawyer will want to use this description in your contract.

If you use dimensions in your listing sheet, be certain that the dimensions which you are offering are those that are contained on your survey. If they are less than you represent them to be, the buyer may easily back out of the contract. All factual statements about the dimensions should come from official instruments such as your survey or your deed.

Make certain that you don't tell the buyer he's getting more than is actually included in the sale. If you point out lot boundaries by trees or fences, be certain that those trees or fences do actually represent your boundary line. If you make a mistake, it could give your buyer grounds to back out of the contract, because you cannot deliver all you said you would.

If you make representations about the condition of the house, be certain that these representations will hold up. You may be required to fix those items you misrepresented.

You also may be selling items of personal property with your house (described in Chapter 3). Since price negotiations often include the addition or subtraction of these "give up" items, you should price these before you offer your house. You will then have established their value for use in bargaining.

These extra items can be important selling tools that you will want to discuss with your buyer. Each item sold should be listed in the sales contract. You will probably be called upon to give a bill of sale for them at closing.

If your house is relatively new, or if you have recently purchased equipment such as a new furnace, there may be an unexpired warranty that the buyer will want transferred at the closing. Your roof may have a twenty-year warranty with ten years left and your appliances may have five-year warranties with three years left. Bring these warranties to the attention of your lawyer so he can indicate them in the contract.

An example of how your property might be described in your sales contract is as follows:

LOT 4, BLOCK 3, OF RED CREEK SUBDIVISION OF THE CITY OF CLEVELAND, OHIO, COMMONLY KNOWN AS 1212 LEGALWAY, CLEVELAND, OHIO, TOGETHER WITH ALL BUILDINGS, INSTALLED FIXTURES, AND OTHER IMPROVEMENTS APPURTENANT THERETO.

INCLUDED IN THIS SALE ARE THE FOLLOWING: ATTACHED TV ANTENNA; SCREENS; STORM WINDOWS; HEATING EQUIPMENT INCLUDING FURNACE; PLUMBING FIXTURES INCLUDING HOT-WATER HEATER; SUMP PUMP; CENTRAL AIR-CONDITIONING EQUIPMENT; BUILT-IN KITCHEN, LAUNDRY, AND BATHROOM CABINETS; WALL-TO-WALL CARPETING, INCLUDING WALL-TO-WALL STAIR CARPETING.

ADDITIONAL PERSONAL PROPERTY INCLUDED IN THIS SALE: STOVE, REFRIGERATOR, AND HALL MIRROR.

UNEXPIRED FURNACE WARRANTY WILL BE ASSIGNED TO PURCHASER AT CLOSING.

In some cities the sales contract will list the items to be removed from the house as well as the items sold. Your lawyer will know the "local custom" and advise you accordingly. If you have valuable antique fixtures such as chandeliers, coach lamps, or sconces, replace these items *before* you show the house to avoid any disputes with the buyer.

AGREEMENT TO BUY AND SELL

The agreement to buy on the part of the buyer and the agreement to sell on the part of the seller is usually the shortest, simplest part of a contact.

THE BUYER AGREES TO BUY AND THE SELLER AGREES TO SELL ON THE TERMS CONTAINED HEREIN, THE DESCRIBED PREMISES AND TO PERFORM ALL OF THE OTHER COVENANTS, UNDERTAKINGS, AND CONDITIONS OF THIS AGREEMENT.

DETERMINE YOUR EARNEST MONEY REQUIREMENTS

Assume your buyer has offered to pay $100,000 for your house. He has $20,000 to put down and will have to find a loan for $80,000 to complete the purchase. You both want to sign a contract today. As the seller, however, you are concerned that the buyer may change his mind. After all, you are going to take your house off the market while he applies for a loan.

To bind your sale, you naturally want the buyer to put up as much earnest money as possible. Customarily, this might be 10 percent of your selling price, or $10,000 in the above example. The buyer would then have to pay dearly if he wanted to back out. The buyer knows this too and will want to put up as little as possible.

There is a middle ground. You can, if you think your deal is solid, take a "good faith deposit" of one-half the full customary earnest money amount, for example, one-half of $10,000 or $5,000. This will be held until the buyer's loan is approved. The buyer will then not have to deplete his savings account, or cash in more stock, until he is certain he can get the loan. When his loan is approved, the buyer would increase his earnest money to the full amount by paying you the additional $5,000.

Buyers are reluctant to give large sums directly to sellers, so these payments are usually made to your lawyer. In most states, lawyers are required by law to hold these funds in a special trust account.

Look at how this example might be written up in your sales contract.

THE PURCHASE PRICE IS:

ONE HUNDRED THOUSAND AND NO/100 . . . $100,000

EARNEST MONEY DELIVERED HEREWITH IS:

FIVE THOUSAND AND NO/100 . . . $5,000

ADDITIONAL EARNEST MONEY TO BE PAID WITHIN FIVE DAYS AFTER BUYER'S LOAN IS APPROVED IS:

FIVE THOUSAND AND NO/100 . . . $5,000

EARNEST MONEY PAYMENTS WILL BE MADE TO SELLER'S LAWYER TO BE HELD BY HIM IN A SPECIAL TRUST ACCOUNT FOR THE BENEFIT OF THE PARTIES. ALL PAYMENTS TO BE MADE IN CASH, CERTIFIED CHECK, OR CASHIER'S CHECK ORIGINALLY DRAWN TO ORDER OF SELLER BY BUYER. BALANCE TO BE PAID SELLER IN CASH AT CLOSING SUBJECT TO PRORATION OF TAXES, INSURANCE, AND ALL OTHER ADJUSTMENTS BETWEEN THE PARTIES.

DETERMINE THE POSSESSION DATE

Possession is usually given at the closing when you receive a check from the buyer and deliver your deed. Your responsibilities for the house are ended and your buyer then takes possession.

You should set your closing and possession date to suit your needs. But sometimes you can't. Your buyer may want possession before closing to save storage or hotel costs. Putting your buyer in possession before closing, changes rights, responsibilities, and bargaining positions. You should not consent to this without the advice of your lawyer. Furthermore, your buyer may find a lot of things he overlooked and may demand you fix them. Ordinarily, a special agreement, much like a lease, is drawn up to cover this situation and to protect you.

The reverse of this can also occur. The buyer may want to

delay possession. If you are about to buy a house, you will need your funds from this sale to pay for your next house. Don't let the buyer try to delay closing. Arrange the closing date you need and stick with it.

However, if you are caught in a bind with two houses and can't speed up the closing on the house you sold, contact your banker about a "turnaround" or "swing" loan to be paid when your sale is closed. This temporary loan will help carry both houses until your first house is closed.

THE MORTGAGE CONTINGENCY CLAUSE

Normally your buyer will not know whether or not he will qualify for a loan. He will hesitate to leave a "good faith" deposit, which may be forfeited, unless he has the assurance it will be refunded if he cannot qualify for the required loan. This is called a "mortgage contingency clause" and frequently appears in sales contracts:

THIS CONTRACT IS SUBJECT TO THE CONDITION THAT WITHIN SEVEN DAYS FROM TODAY THE BUYER WILL BE ABLE TO OBTAIN A FIRM LOAN COMMITMENT ON THE PREMISES, SECURED BY A TRUST DEED OR MORTGAGE IN THE AMOUNT OF $80,000 (OR SUCH LESS SUM AS A BUYER WILL ACCEPT), REPAYABLE WITH INTEREST AT 10 PERCENT PER ANNUM TO BE AMORTIZED OVER TWENTY-FIVE YEARS, THE SERVICE CHARGE TO THE BUYER FOR SUCH LOAN NOT TO EXCEED 2 PERCENT OF THE PRINCIPAL AMOUNT THEREOF.

IF AFTER MAKING EVERY REASONABLE GOOD FAITH EFFORT TO OBTAIN SUCH FINANCING THE BUYER IS DECLINED BY AT LEAST TWO LENDING INSTITUTIONS, BUYER MAY NOTIFY SELLER OF HIS INABILITY TO OBTAIN SUCH FIRM LOAN COMMITMENT. SELLER WILL THEN CAUSE THE BUYER'S DEPOSIT TO BE

REFUNDED IN FULL AT ONCE AND THIS AGREEMENT WILL BE TERMINATED. IF BUYER FAILS TO NOTIFY SELLER OF HIS INABILITY TO OBTAIN SUCH FINANCING, HE SHALL BE PRESUMED EITHER TO HAVE OBTAINED SATISFACTORY FINANCING, OR TO HAVE ELECTED TO PROCEED WITHOUT FINANCING.

The special terms of the above paragraphs should be drawn by your lawyer but you should advise him of the financing data you have gathered on your Mortgage Shopper's guides. This data will be a valuable aid to you and your lawyer in determining the acceptability of the current interest rate, loan amount, and term of the loan specified in the contingency clause.

In completing the Mortgage Shopper's Guides you will have determined the average processing time that the lending institutions will need from application by the buyer to the date they will commit for a loan. Maker certain the "mortgage contingency clause" specifies the shortest possible (and yet still reasonable) period of time. For example, if the average processing time, as determined by your telephone survey, is seven days, consider allowing no more than eight or nine days in your sales contract. It would be unwise to allow two or three weeks and lose this valuable marketing time while your house is off the market and your buyer is shopping for a loan commitment.

The FHA and VA demand that the buyer get his deposit back if he cannot obtain a loan. FHA and VA financing also take much longer for approval than conventional financing. Two weeks will never be enough to process a loan application. If you think you will be involved in federally insured financing, your house should be appraised by an FHA or VA appraiser before you offer it for sale. This early FHA or VA authorized appraisal will speed up the processing considerably.

If you plan to sell your house within FHA price guidelines, you will want to know if the buyer can qualify for an insured

FHA loan. Your contract should contain an agreement that the buyer's credit rating be satisfactory for such a loan or that you be advised of this within two weeks of the time you sign the contract.

THE "SUBJECT TO SALE" CONTINGENCY

The situation frequently arises where a seller has reached agreement with a buyer, but the buyer must sell his own house before he can purchase the seller's house. He wants to buy, but can't promise to purchase until he has sold his own house. To solve his dilemma he submits a contract conditioned on the sale of his house within, for example, sixty days.

What should you do? Refuse the contract or accept? Consider accepting his contract under the following condition: you will continue to offer your house for sale on the market, and if you find a second buyer, your first buyer will have forty-eight hours to eliminate the "subject to sale" contingency from his contract. If he doesn't, his contract will be automatically canceled and you have the right to enter into a firm sales contract with your new buyer. Get your lawyer's advice if your buyer suggests this contingency.

SPECIAL ASSESSMENTS

Special assessments for improvements such as streetlights, paving, or sewers are customarily paid by the seller at closing. The buyer is buying the property with these improvements already in place and he will not expect to pay extra for them. Unpaid installments of these assessments frequently constitute

liens against the property and many lenders object to them.
Your best guide for the treatment of these items will be your
lawyer. He can tell you how they are handled in your
community.

TITLE EVIDENCE, DEED, AND CLOSING DOCUMENTS

A "title" is not a physical document but rather the
evidence of ownership as represented by many documents.
The specific document that will be used to convey your title is
the "deed" that you will give to your buyer. Your buyer will
want to know if you have good and clear title to your house
when you deliver your deed.

Your buyer's lawyer will examine the history and evidence of your title (abstract) or have a title company issue a
certificate of title or a title insurance policy. The title insurance
policy will guarantee that you have good and clear title before
the buyer takes your deed. If your title is not in "marketable"
condition your buyer will not have to accept it. If this occurs,
your lawyer can help by suggesting and negotiating solutions
to this situation.

While your contract looks to your title evidence and deed
as the primary closing documents, there are a host of additional
supporting documents that your buyer may request:

AFFIDAVIT OF TITLE. A STATEMENT UNDER OATH THAT THE PROPERTY IS FREE
OF LIENS AND ENCUMBRANCES OTHER THAN THOSE SHOWN IN THE TITLE
EVIDENCE.

PLAT OF SURVEY. A MAP DRAWN BY A LICENSED SURVEYOR WHO HAS
SURVEYED THE PROPERTY, SHOWING THE LOT DIMENSIONS AND LOCATING
THE IMPROVEMENTS IN THE PROPERTY, EASEMENTS, AND RECORDED

BUILDING LINES. THESE CAN BE EITHER INEXPENSIVE OR VERY COSTLY SO
SPECIFY IN YOUR CONTRACT WHETHER THE SURVEY IS TO BE PROVIDED BY
YOU OR BY THE BUYER.

BILL OF SALE. AN INSTRUMENT OF TRANSFER OF PERSONAL PROPERTY OR
CONTRACTUAL RIGHTS (SUCH AS LEASES, INSURANCE POLICIES, WARRAN-
TIES).

AFFIDAVITS. MISCELLANEOUS AFFIDAVITS TO COVER SPECIFIC TITLE MATTERS.
THE VARIETY OF THESE IS ALMOST INFINITE.

CLOSING STATEMENT. AN ITEMIZATION OF THE AMOUNTS OWED EACH OF THE
PARTIES. THE CLOSING STATEMENT RECONCILES ALL THE VARIOUS CREDITS
BETWEEN YOU AND THE SELLER SUCH AS TAXES, INSURANCE, FUEL, AND
WATER. THE CLOSING STATEMENT INDICATES THE NET AMOUNT THE BUYER
WILL OWE YOU AT THE TIME OF CLOSING.

TRANSFER NOTICES. TAXING AUTHORITIES AND PUBLIC UTILITIES ARE
USUALLY NOTIFIED TO SEND BILLS TO THE NEW OWNERS.

MISCELLANEOUS DOCUMENTS. LOCALLY REQUIRED GOVERNMENTAL DOCU-
MENTS, TRANSFER TAX STATEMENTS, OCCUPANCY PERMITS, NOTICES OF
ZONING COMPLIANCE, AND BUILDING DEPARTMENT CERTIFICATES, IF RE-
QUIRED, ARE DELIVERED AT THE CLOSING.

GENERAL AND SPECIAL AGREEMENTS

General and special agreements cover some of the basic
items to be included in your sales contract. Agreements must
be reached on several possible circumstances. What happens if
the closing must be delayed? What happens if a fire occurs
before the closing? Can the buyer back out or must you repair
the damage, and at what cost? Will the buyer require a
warranty that the heating, air-conditioning, and plumbing
fixtures are in good working order? Must you give the city
building department a certificate of occupancy?

These questions, and many others, will be answered by

your lawyer. He will advise you of problem areas and will know how to handle them according to the local real estate law, the "local custom," and your specific requirements.

THE BINDER

In some states it is local custom for a buyer and seller to sign a document called a "binder." The principal purpose of the binder is for the buyer and seller to enter into a "preliminary" agreement that sets forth the price and basic terms of the sale. A buyer normally signs a binder in order to take the house off the market over a weekend. A seller can use a binder as a sales tool to get the buyer's consent in writing to the price and the basic terms until a more formal sales contract can be drawn up by the lawyers.

Neither the buyer nor the seller expects that he will be legally bound when he signs a binder. Both feel the only purpose of the binder is to hold the deal together until their lawyers can draw up a more definitive sales contract.

Unfortunately, it sometimes happens that either the lawyers cannot get the parties to agree on the detailed terms of a formal sales contract or one of the parties decides not to go through with the deal. When this occurs, a serious problem can arise. What was originally thought to be only a "preliminary" document can now be held to be legally binding and then the fight begins.

If it is local custom in your area to use a binder, be on the safe side and consult with your lawyer. Ask him to draw up a binder that will help you and your buyer arrive at a "preliminary" agreement but will avoid difficult legal problems if the deal falls through. (A blank sample binder is shown on the opposite page.)

BINDER

Agreement, Between _____ and purchaser subscribing hereto. Purchaser agrees to purchase _____

at price of $ _____ with a deposit of $ _____ for which this is a receipt, and $ _____ when a more formal contract, such as is used by Title Companies, is signed by owner and purchaser, which is to be signed within _____ days, at _____. When warranty deed is delivered on _____ 19 ___ at _____ the purchaser agrees to pay $ _____, and $ _____ by assuming and agreeing to pay mortgage for that amount now on property above described. Balance $ _____ to be paid by purchaser _____

_____. In case the owner is not willing to accept the amount and terms as outlined above, the deposit is to be returned. If owner accepts and purchaser fails to comply, deposit shall be forfeited.

_____

_____

Above agreement approved and accepted by owner, who agrees to pay _____ _____ % of the purchase price as commission.

Broker _____

_____ _____ _Purchaser_

Owner _____

_____ _Purchaser Address_

(Reproduced with permission of S. S. Clarkson Mfg. Corp., Brooklyn, N.Y.)

CHECK LIST
HOW YOUR LAWYER WILL HELP YOUR SALE

☐ HIRE A LAWYER EXPERIENCED IN HOME SALES

☐ THE SALES CONTRACT

☐ MAKE CERTAIN ALL PARTIES SIGN THE CONTRACT

☐ PROPERLY DESCRIBE YOUR PROPERTY

☐ AGREEMENT TO BUY AND SELL

☐ DETERMINE YOUR EARNEST MONEY REQUIREMENTS

☐ DETERMINE THE POSSESSION DATE

☐ THE MORTGAGE CONTINGENCY CLAUSE

☐ THE "SUBJECT TO SALE" CONTINGENCY

☐ SPECIAL ASSESSMENTS

☐ TITLE EVIDENCE, DEED, AND CLOSING DOCUMENTS

☐ GENERAL AND SPECIAL AGREEMENTS

CHAPTER
8

FOR SALE

HOW TO WORK WITH REAL ESTATE BROKERS

BY OWNER

As soon as you place your house on the market you will undoubtedly be contacted by several real estate brokers. Some may tell you that they have qualified buyers ready to purchase your house, if *only* you will sign a listing contract. Some may be certain that they can sell your house immediately . . . if *only* you will sign a listing contract.

When one of these brokers informs you that he has your buyer, you can express delight, but *do not* sign a listing contract. If you sign, based on the broker's expectation that he can find a buyer, you may have been caught by his sales pitch and may as well forget "For Sale by Owner." You will pay a full commission, *when* and *if* he finds a buyer. It may take the full six months of the listing contract for him to succeed.

Assume that the broker insists he has a buyer willing to purchase your house right now for the asking price. In this situation, you may be willing to pay full commission in return for an immediate sale. Tell the broker that you will sign a listing contract allowing him to show the house only to a specific individual to be named in the contract. The contract should state that you will pay the commission only on the condition that the individual named purchases the house. Most brokers will back off since they may not actually have a buyer ready but are simply attempting to persuade you to sign a three- or six-month listing contract.

You *can* work with a broker and still save a portion of the commission. To accomplish this, you must first understand how the commission structure works. If you list your house with broker A and broker A finds the buyer, broker A receives the full commission (for example, 6 percent). If you list your house with broker A and broker B finds the buyer, broker A and broker B would split the commission. Normally the listing broker will receive a slightly larger share of the total commission than the broker who finds the buyer. For example, broker A might receive 3½ percent and broker B might receive 2½ percent. This will vary from city to city depending on local custom.

Assume you determine the "fair market value" of your house is $120,000. Then you raise the $120,000 "fair market value" to an asking price of $128,000. You can still work with a real estate broker and save money. Based on the above assumption your goal is to receive a net of $120,000. You can let a broker show your house and still not sign a listing contract. Inform the broker that if the house is sold to any client that he shows through the house, you will pay his 2½ percent commission (or the normal split that he would receive if the house had been listed by another real estate broker). Also inform the broker that you will consider any *offers,* but *don't* tell him what price you will accept. If he knows your net price he may be tempted to tell the buyer. The buyer may then bid lower than your net price. You may find yourself backed into a corner, forced to compromise below your net price. Stick to your asking price in all discussions with the broker, and request that his buyer submit a written contract that you will either accept, reject, or counter.

In the above example, if a broker has not been involved, you could accept a bid of $120,000 and receive your full net price. However, with the broker involved, you will have to pay 2½ percent commission. To still receive your full net price of $120,000, and also pay a 2½ percent commissioin, you have to raise the price you will accept by the amount of the commission. If you raise the price you will accept to $123,000, you can pay a 2½ percent commission of $3,000 (exactly $3075), and still receive close to your net of $120,000.

If you can't raise your price to cover the commission, it still may be feasible to work with a broker that has a qualified buyer. If your final price is $120,000, you will pay 2½ percent or $3,000 commission but still will save the other 3½ percent or $4,200. The $3,000 may be well spent if the broker delivers a qualified buyer in a reasonable period of time, and if you have not tied yourself down with a listing contract.

Another approach is to inform the broker that you have decided to sell your own house, and, if the broker is to receive a commission, he must receive it from the buyer. You may find brokers who are willing to work with prospective buyers and receive the commission from them.

If you have a saleable house in a good real estate market, the best position to take during the early stages of selling your house is to inform the broker that you have no intention of selling through a broker. Most brokers will then stop calling. If you change your mind at a later date you will have no difficulty finding a broker to represent you.

Whether you work with a broker on a split-commission or a full-commission basis, you must understand the broker's share of the sale price in relation to your share of the sale price.

Assume you have an asking price of $128,000, a "fair market value" of $120,000, and a minimum price of $110,000. If you disclose your minimum price to a broker he may recommend that the buyer submit an offer of $110,000 with an expected counter offer of $115,000. He knows both your minimum and the buyer's maximum, and he hopes to strike a deal. One broker may be representing you (if you have a listing contract) and another broker from the same real estate company may find a buyer. It is to both brokers' advantage to work with both the buyer and seller and close the transaction as soon as possible. The brokers are in a commission business where turnover is an important factor in determining their annual income.

In the above example, assume you are convinced by your broker to counter the offer of $110,000 and then accept $115,000. What have you lost and what has the broker lost by dropping down to $115,000 from your "fair market value" of $120,000? You have lost $4,700! The broker has lost $300!

At a $120,000 selling price your net proceeds are $120,000 minus 6 percent commission or $112,800. At a $115,000 selling price your net proceeds are $115,000 minus 6 percent commission or $108,100. The difference in your net proceeds is $4,700.

At a $120,000 selling price the broker's net proceeds are $120,000 times 6 percent commission or $7,200. At a $115,000 selling price the broker's net proceeds are $115,000 times 6 percent commission or $6,900. The difference in his commission is $300.

Whenever you work with a broker, calculate the effect of a drop in price on him, and the effect on you. Even though he may be representing you, look at the stakes involved. A suggestion to accept a $115,000 offer costs you $4,700 and the broker $300! Your loss is substantially higher than the broker's loss. Does it make good sense to disclose your minimum and net price to the broker and then turn the negotiations over to him? Or, do you prefer "For Sale by Owner"?

APPENDIX
1

MORTGAGE LOAN
TABLES

The mortgage loan tables in Appendix 1 are limited in percentage range, number of years, and loan amounts. They have also been rounded to whole dollars. While care has been taken, there is no guarantee that they do not contain errors. It is recommended that your buyer obtain a mortgage payment book from a lending institution to ensure complete accuracy.

MONTHLY PAYMENT
NECESSARY TO AMORTIZE A LOAN · 9%

Amount	15 yrs.	20 yrs.	25 yrs.	30 yrs.	35 yrs.
20,000	203	180	168	161	157
25,000	254	225	210	201	196
30,000	304	270	252	241	235
35,000	355	315	294	282	274
36,000	365	324	302	290	282
37,000	375	333	311	298	290
38,000	385	342	319	306	298
39,000	396	351	327	314	306
40,000	406	360	336	322	314
41,000	416	369	344	330	321
42,000	426	378	352	338	329
43,000	436	387	361	346	337
44,000	446	396	369	354	345
45,000	456	405	378	362	353
46,000	467	414	386	370	361
47,000	477	423	394	378	368
48,000	487	432	403	386	376
49,000	497	441	411	394	384
50,000	507	450	420	402	392
51,000	517	459	428	418	400
52,000	527	468	436	426	408
53,000	538	477	445	435	416
54,000	548	486	453	443	423
55,000	558	495	462	451	431
60,000	609	540	503	483	470
65,000	659	585	545	523	510
70,000	710	630	587	563	549
75,000	761	675	629	603	588
80,000	811	720	671	644	627
85,000	862	765	713	684	666
90,000	913	810	755	724	706
95,000	964	855	797	764	745
100,000	1014	900	839	805	784

MONTHLY PAYMENT
NECESSARY TO AMORTIZE A LOAN 9½%

Amount	15 yrs.	20 yrs.	25 yrs.	30 yrs.	35 yrs.
20,000	209	186	175	168	164
25,000	261	233	218	210	205
30,000	313	280	263	252	246
35,000	365	326	306	294	287
36,000	376	336	315	303	296
37,000	386	345	323	311	304
38,000	397	354	332	320	312
39,000	407	364	341	328	320
40,000	418	373	349	336	329
41,000	428	382	358	345	336
42,000	439	392	367	353	345
43,000	449	401	376	362	353
44,000	459	410	384	370	361
45,000	470	419	393	378	370
46,000	480	429	402	387	378
47,000	491	438	411	395	386
48,000	501	447	419	403	394
49,000	512	457	428	412	403
50,000	522	466	437	420	411
51,000	533	475	446	429	419
52,000	543	485	454	437	427
53,000	553	494	463	446	435
54,000	564	503	472	454	444
55,000	574	513	481	462	452
60,000	627	559	524	505	493
65,000	679	606	568	547	534
70,000	731	653	612	589	575
75,000	783	699	655	631	616
80,000	835	746	699	673	657
85,000	888	792	743	715	698
90,000	940	839	786	757	739
95,000	992	886	830	799	781
100,000	1044	932	874	841	822

MONTHLY PAYMENT
NECESSARY TO AMORTIZE A LOAN 10%

Amount	15 yrs.	20 yrs.	25 yrs.	30 yrs.	35 yrs.
20,000	215	193	182	176	172
25,000	269	241	227	219	215
30,000	322	290	273	263	258
35,000	376	338	318	307	301
36,000	387	347	327	316	309
37,000	398	357	336	325	318
38,000	408	367	345	333	327
39,000	419	376	354	342	335
40,000	430	386	363	351	344
41,000	441	396	373	360	352
42,000	451	405	382	369	361
43,000	462	415	391	377	370
44,000	473	425	400	386	378
45,000	484	434	409	395	387
46,000	494	444	418	404	395
47,000	505	454	427	412	404
48,000	516	463	436	421	413
49,000	527	472	445	430	421
50,000	537	483	454	439	430
51,000	548	492	463	448	438
52,000	559	502	473	456	447
53,000	570	511	482	465	456
54,000	580	521	491	474	464
55,000	591	531	500	483	473
60,000	645	579	545	527	516
65,000	698	627	591	570	559
70,000	752	676	636	614	602
75,000	806	724	682	658	645
80,000	860	772	727	702	688
85,000	913	820	772	746	731
90,000	967	869	818	790	774
95,000	1021	917	863	834	817
100,000	1075	965	909	878	860

MONTHLY PAYMENT
NECESSARY TO AMORTIZE A LOAN 10½%

Amount	15 yrs.	20 yrs.	25 yrs.	30 yrs.	35 yrs.
20,000	221	200	189	183	180
25,000	276	250	236	229	225
30,000	332	300	283	274	269
35,000	387	349	330	320	314
36,000	398	359	340	329	323
37,000	404	369	349	338	332
38,000	420	379	359	348	341
39,000	431	389	368	357	350
40,000	442	399	378	366	359
41,000	453	409	387	375	368
42,000	464	419	397	384	377
43,000	475	429	406	393	386
44,000	486	439	415	402	395
45,000	497	449	425	412	409
46,000	508	459	434	421	413
47,000	520	469	444	430	422
48,000	531	479	453	439	431
49,000	542	489	463	448	440
50,000	553	499	472	457	449
51,000	564	509	482	467	458
52,000	575	519	491	476	467
53,000	586	529	500	485	476
54,000	597	539	510	494	484
55,000	608	549	519	503	493
60,000	663	599	567	549	539
65,000	719	649	614	595	584
70,000	774	699	661	640	629
75,000	829	749	708	686	674
80,000	884	799	755	732	719
85,000	940	849	803	778	763
90,000	995	899	850	823	808
95,000	1050	948	897	869	853
100,000	1105	998	944	915	898

MONTHLY PAYMENT
NECESSARY TO AMORTIZE A LOAN 11%

Amount	15 yrs.	20 yrs.	25 yrs.	30 yrs.	35 yrs.
20,000	227	206	196	190	186
25,000	284	258	245	238	234
30,000	341	310	294	286	281
35,000	398	361	343	333	328
36,000	409	372	353	343	337
37,000	421	382	363	353	347
38,000	432	392	372	362	356
39,000	443	403	382	371	365
40,000	455	413	392	381	375
41,000	466	423	402	390	384
42,000	477	434	412	400	394
43,000	489	444	422	410	403
44,000	500	454	432	419	412
45,000	511	464	441	429	422
46,000	523	475	451	438	431
47,000	534	485	461	448	440
48,000	546	495	470	457	450
49,000	557	506	480	467	459
50,000	568	516	490	476	468
51,000	580	526	500	486	478
52,000	591	537	510	495	487
53,000	602	547	519	505	496
54,000	614	557	529	514	506
55,000	625	568	539	524	515
60,000	682	619	588	571	562
65,000	784	671	637	619	609
70,000	796	723	686	667	656
75,000	852	774	735	714	703
80,000	909	826	784	762	750
85,000	966	877	833	809	796
90,000	1023	929	882	857	843
95,000	1080	981	931	905	890
100,000	1137	1032	980	952	937

MONTHLY PAYMENT
NECESSARY TO AMORTIZE A LOAN 11½%

Amount	15 yrs.	20 yrs.	25 yrs.	30 yrs.	35 yrs.
20,000	234	213	203	198	195
25,000	292	267	252	248	244
30,000	350	310	305	297	293
35,000	409	373	356	347	342
36,000	421	384	366	357	351
37,000	432	395	376	366	361
38,000	444	405	386	376	371
39,000	456	416	396	386	381
40,000	467	427	407	396	390
41,000	479	437	417	406	400
42,000	490	448	427	416	410
43,000	502	459	437	426	420
44,000	514	469	447	436	429
45,000	526	480	457	446	439
46,000	537	491	468	456	449
47,000	549	501	478	465	459
48,000	560	512	488	475	468
49,000	572	523	498	485	478
50,000	584	533	508	495	488
51,000	596	544	518	505	498
52,000	607	555	528	515	508
53,000	619	565	539	525	517
54,000	630	576	549	535	527
55,000	643	587	559	545	537
60,000	701	640	610	594	586
65,000	759	693	661	644	634
70,000	818	747	712	693	683
75,000	876	800	762	743	732
80,000	935	853	813	792	781
85,000	993	906	864	842	830
90,000	1051	960	915	891	878
95,000	1110	1013	966	941	927
100,000	1168	1066	1016	990	976

MONTHLY PAYMENT
NECESSARY TO AMORTIZE A LOAN 12%

Amount	15 yrs.	20 yrs.	25 yrs.	30 yrs.	35 yrs.
20,000	240	220	211	206	203
25,000	300	275	263	257	254
30,000	360	330	316	309	305
35,000	420	385	369	360	355
36,000	432	396	379	370	366
37,000	444	407	390	381	376
38,000	456	418	400	391	386
39,000	468	429	411	401	396
40,000	480	440	421	411	406
41,000	492	451	432	422	416
42,000	504	462	442	432	427
43,000	516	473	453	442	437
44,000	528	484	463	453	447
45,000	540	495	474	463	457
46,000	552	506	484	473	467
47,000	564	518	495	483	477
48,000	576	529	506	494	487
49,000	588	539	517	504	498
50,000	600	551	527	514	508
51,000	612	562	537	524	518
52,000	624	573	548	535	528
53,000	636	584	558	545	538
54,000	648	595	569	555	548
55,000	660	606	579	566	559
60,000	720	661	632	617	609
65,000	780	716	685	669	660
70,000	840	771	737	720	711
75,000	900	826	790	771	762
80,000	960	881	843	823	812
85,000	1020	936	895	874	863
90,000	1080	991	948	926	914
95,000	1140	1046	1001	977	965
100,000	1200	1101	1053	1029	1016

MONTHLY PAYMENT
NECESSARY TO AMORTIZE A LOAN 12½%

Amount	15 yrs.	20 yrs.	25 yrs.	30 yrs.	35 yrs.
20,000	247	227	218	213	211
25,000	308	284	273	267	264
30,000	370	341	327	320	317
35,000	431	398	382	374	369
36,000	443	409	393	384	380
37,000	456	420	403	395	390
38,000	468	432	414	406	401
39,000	481	443	425	416	412
40,000	493	454	436	427	422
41,000	505	465	447	438	433
42,000	517	476	458	449	443
43,000	529	487	469	459	454
44,000	542	499	480	470	465
45,000	555	511	491	480	475
46,000	567	522	501	491	485
47,000	579	533	511	502	495
48,000	592	545	522	512	506
49,000	605	557	533	523	517
50,000	616	568	545	534	528
51,000	628	579	556	544	538
52,000	640	590	567	554	548
53,000	653	602	578	565	559
54,000	665	613	589	576	569
55,000	678	625	600	587	580
60,000	740	682	654	640	633
65,000	801	738	709	694	686
70,000	863	795	763	747	739
75,000	924	852	818	800	791
80,000	986	909	872	854	844
85,000	1048	966	927	907	897
90,000	1109	1023	981	961	950
95,000	1171	1079	1021	1014	1002
100,000	1233	1136	1075	1067	1055

MONTHLY PAYMENT
NECESSARY TO AMORTIZE A LOAN   13%

Amount	15 yrs.	20 yrs.	25 yrs.	30 yrs.	35 yrs.
20,000	253	234	226	221	219
25,000	316	293	282	277	274
30,000	380	351	338	332	329
35,000	443	410	395	387	383
36,000	455	422	406	398	394
37,000	468	433	417	409	405
38,000	481	445	429	420	416
39,000	493	457	440	431	427
40,000	506	469	451	443	438
41,000	518	480	462	454	448
42,000	530	491	473	465	458
43,000	543	503	485	476	469
44,000	556	515	497	487	480
45,000	569	527	508	498	492
46,000	581	538	519	509	503
47,000	593	549	530	520	514
48,000	606	561	542	531	525
49,000	619	573	554	542	537
50,000	633	586	564	553	548
51,000	646	597	575	564	558
52,000	658	608	586	575	569
53,000	671	620	597	586	580
54,000	684	632	609	597	591
55,000	696	644	620	608	602
60,000	759	703	677	664	657
65,000	822	762	733	719	712
70,000	886	820	789	774	767
75,000	949	879	846	830	821
80,000	1012	937	902	885	876
85,000	1075	996	959	940	931
90,000	1139	1054	1015	996	985
95,000	1202	1113	1071	1051	1040
100,000	1265	1172	1128	1106	1095

MONTHLY PAYMENT
NECESSARY TO AMORTIZE A LOAN 13½%

Amount	15 yrs.	20 yrs.	25 yrs.	30 yrs.	35 yrs.
20,000	260	241	233	229	227
25,000	325	302	291	286	284
30,000	390	362	350	344	341
35,000	454	423	408	401	397
36,000	467	435	420	412	409
37,000	480	447	431	424	420
38,000	493	459	443	435	431
39,000	506	471	455	447	443
40,000	519	483	466	458	454
41,000	532	495	477	469	465
42,000	545	507	489	481	476
43,000	558	519	501	492	488
44,000	571	531	512	503	500
45,000	584	543	525	515	511
46,000	597	555	536	526	522
47,000	610	567	548	538	533
48,000	623	580	559	549	545
49,000	636	592	571	560	557
50,000	649	604	583	573	568
51,000	662	616	594	584	579
52,000	675	628	605	595	590
53,000	688	640	617	607	602
54,000	701	652	629	619	614
55,000	714	664	641	630	624
60,000	779	724	699	687	681
65,000	844	785	758	745	738
70,000	909	845	816	802	795
75,000	974	906	874	859	852
80,000	1039	966	933	916	908
85,000	1104	1026	991	974	965
90,000	1168	1087	1049	1031	1022
95,000	1233	1147	1107	1088	1079
100,000	1298	1207	1166	1145	1135

MONTHLY PAYMENT
NECESSARY TO AMORTIZE A LOAN 14%

Amount	15 yrs.	20 yrs.	25 yrs.	30 yrs.	35 yrs.
20,000	266	249	241	237	235
25,000	333	311	301	296	294
30,000	400	373	361	355	353
35,000	466	435	421	415	411
36,000	479	448	433	427	423
37,000	493	460	445	438	435
38,000	506	473	457	450	447
39,000	519	485	469	462	459
40,000	533	497	482	474	470
41,000	546	509	494	485	481
42,000	559	522	506	497	492
43,000	572	535	518	509	504
44,000	585	548	530	521	516
45,000	599	560	542	533	529
46,000	612	572	554	544	540
47,000	626	585	566	555	552
48,000	639	598	578	567	563
49,000	652	610	590	579	575
50,000	666	622	602	592	588
51,000	679	634	614	604	599
52,000	692	647	626	616	611
53,000	706	660	638	628	622
54,000	719	672	650	640	634
55,000	732	684	662	652	647
60,000	799	746	722	711	705
65,000	866	808	782	770	764
70,000	932	870	843	829	823
75,000	999	933	903	889	882
80,000	1065	995	963	948	941
85,000	1131	1057	1023	1007	999
90,000	1199	1119	1083	1066	1058
95,000	1265	1181	1144	1126	1117
100,000	1332	1244	1204	1185	1176

APPENDIX
2

BLANK FORMS

FOR SALE BY OWNER

OWNER	
RES. PHONE	
BUS. PHONE	

ADDRESS		COMMUNITY	ROOMS	BDRMS	BATH	PRICE
STYLE		PATIO				
CONSTRUCTION		FIREPLACE				
AGE		CARPETS				
LOT SIZE		DRAPES				
SQ. FT.		HEAT				
LIVING RM.		AIR COND				
DINING RM.		DISHWASHER				
FAMILY RM.		DISPOSAL				
BEDROOM 1		STOVE				
BEDROOM 2		CITY WATER				
BEDROOM 3		SEWER				
BEDROOM 4		PROPERTY TAX				
BEDROOM 5		SCHOOL: ELEM.				
KITCHEN		J.H.S.				
BREAKFAST RM.		H.S.				
BASEMENT						
GARAGE						
CLOSETS						

FOR SALE
BY OWNER

OWNER
RES. PHONE
BUS. PHONE

ADDRESS	COMMUNITY	ROOMS	BDRMS	BATH	PRICE
STYLE		PATIO			
CONSTRUCTION		FIREPLACE			
AGE		CARPETS			
LOT SIZE		DRAPES			
SQ. FT.		HEAT			
LIVING RM.		AIR COND			
DINING RM.		DISHWASHER			
FAMILY RM.		DISPOSAL			
BEDROOM 1		STOVE			
BEDROOM 2		CITY WATER			
BEDROOM 3		SEWER			
BEDROOM 4		PROPERTY TAX			
BEDROOM 5		SCHOOL: ELEM.			
KITCHEN		J.H.S.			
BREAKFAST RM.		H.S.			
BASEMENT					
GARAGE					
CLOSETS					

FOR SALE BY OWNER

OWNER
RES. PHONE
BUS. PHONE

ADDRESS	COMMUNITY	ROOMS	BDRMS	BATH	PRICE
STYLE		PATIO			
CONSTRUCTION		FIREPLACE			
AGE		CARPETS			
LOT SIZE		DRAPES			
SQ. FT.		HEAT			
LIVING RM.		AIR COND			
DINING RM.		DISHWASHER			
FAMILY RM.		DISPOSAL			
BEDROOM 1		STOVE			
BEDROOM 2		CITY WATER			
BEDROOM 3		SEWER			
BEDROOM 4		PROPERTY TAX			
BEDROOM 5		SCHOOL: ELEM.			
KITCHEN		J.H.S.			
BREAKFAST RM.		H.S.			
BASEMENT					
GARAGE					
CLOSETS					

FOR SALE
BY OWNER

OWNER	
ADDRESS	
RES. PHONE	
BUS. PHONE	

EXPENSES

ITEMS INCLUDED WITH HOUSE

FOR SALE
BY OWNER

OWNER	
ADDRESS	
RES. PHONE	
BUS. PHONE	

EXPENSES

ITEMS INCLUDED WITH HOUSE

FOR SALE
BY OWNER

OWNER	
ADDRESS	
RES. PHONE	
BUS. PHONE	

EXPENSES

ITEMS INCLUDED WITH HOUSE

FOR SALE BY OWNER

OWNER
ADDRESS
RES. PHONE
BUS. PHONE

Month	Elec.	Gas	Water	Sewer	Refuse	
Total						
Av. Mo.						

FOR SALE BY OWNER

OWNER	
ADDRESS	
RES. PHONE	
BUS. PHONE	

Month	Elec.	Gas	Water	Sewer	Refuse	
Total						
Av. Mo.						

FOR SALE
BY OWNER

| OWNER |
| ADDRESS |
| RES. PHONE |
| BUS. PHONE |

Month	Elec.	Gas	Water	Sewer	Refuse	
Total						
Av. Mo.						

FOR SALE
BY OWNER

OWNER
ADDRESS
RES. PHONE
BUS. PHONE

Month	Elec.	Gas	Water	Sewer	Refuse	
Total						
Av. Mo.						

FOR SALE
BY OWNER

OWNER
ADDRESS
RES. PHONE
BUS. PHONE

Month	Elec.	Gas	Water	Sewer	Refuse	
Total						
Av. Mo.						

FOR SALE
BY OWNER

OWNER	
ADDRESS	
RES. PHONE	
BUS. PHONE	

Month	Elec.	Gas	Water	Sewer	Refuse	
Total						
Av. Mo.						